The Southern Way

Colin Scott-Morton

50 Years of the Bournemouth Electrics
1967 to 2017

Special Issue 16

www.crecy.co.uk

© 2019 Colin Scott-Morton

ISBN 9781909328914

First published in 2019 by Noodle Books

New contact details
All editorial submissions to:
The Southern Way (Kevin Robertson)
'Silmaril'
Upper Lambourn
Hungerford
Berkshire RG17 8QR
Tel: 01488 674143
editorial@thesouthernway.co.uk

All rights reserved. No part of this book may be reproduced or transmitted in any form or by any means electronic or mechanical, including photocopying, recording or by any information storage without permission from the Publisher in writing. All enquiries should be directed to the Publisher.

A CIP record for this book is available from the British Library.

Publisher's note: Every effort has been made to identify and correctly attribute photographic credits. Any error that may have occurred is entirely unintentional.

Printed in Malta by Gutenberg

Noodle Books is an imprint of
Crécy Publishing Limited
1a Ringway Trading Estate
Shadowmoss Road
Manchester M22 5LH

www.crecy.co.uk

Issue No 49 of THE SOUTHERN WAY
ISBN 9781909328945
available in January 2020 at £14.95

To receive your copy the moment it is released, order in advance from your usual supplier, or it can be sent post-free (UK) direct from the publisher:

Crécy Publishing Ltd (Noodle Books)

1a Ringway Trading Estate, Shadowmoss Road, Manchester M22 5LH

Tel 0161 499 0024

www.crecy.co.uk

enquiries@crecy.co.uk

Front cover:
Changing times at Bournemouth. Steam is still active on the shed, but its replacement looms large in the foreground in the shape of brand new 4-REP unit 3003. The picture is undated, but 3003 first reached Bournemouth in March 1967. It is seen here in one of the newly commissioned sidings at the western end of the station, and the 'dropped' buckeye coupler suggests that it has either been – or is about to be – attached to a locomotive. *G Pratt/Colour-Rail.com 237314*

Rear cover:
Bournemouth electrics 2015 style. On 18 June, Class 444 'Desiro' unit 444 039 leads an unidentified sister unit through the rhododendron-lined cutting at Winchfield with the 09.03 Weymouth to Waterloo service. The tall Old Potbridge Road overbridge in the background was a feature of many steam-era shots at this location. The lower bridge in front carries the M3 motorway across the line. *Author*

Contents

Acknowledgments 4

Introduction 5

1 Overview 6

2 Track, Signalling, Electrification and Other Works 10

3 Rolling Stock 22

4 1967 42

5 The REP/TC Years 51

6 On to Weymouth 65

7 Clapham 85

8 South Hampshire 90

9 Towards Privatisation 98

10 South West Trains 103

11 Into the New Millennium 110

12 The Desiro Era 117

13 What Next? 136

Appendices 137

Bibliography 141

Index 142

Acknowledgements

I owe a debt of gratitude to a number of people and organisations who have provided me with valuable help, advice, information, and access to excellent photographic collections. Without them, this book would have been a less comprehensive account than it is, or may not have come to fruition at all:

To Kevin Robertson, for his positive encouragement and for guiding me through the complexities of the publishing process;

To Terry Phillips, for his meticulous proof-reading of the manuscript, and for providing constructive feedback on both the linguistic style and technical content;

To John Atkinson, John H Bird, Barry S Doe, Colin J Marsden, John Scrace, Christopher J Wilson, the National Archives, the National Railway Museum, and the Transport Treasury;

And last – but by no means least – to my wife Fiona, for her patience and support throughout the process.

Colin Scott-Morton

Introduction

The electrification of the railways in Southern England has been well documented in many excellent publications elsewhere, and a detailed history is outside the scope of this book. However, a brief summary will probably help to put what follows in context.

The London and South Western and the London, Brighton and South Coast railway companies had started electrifying their London suburban lines before the First World War, and this process continued after they were grouped, along with the South Eastern and Chatham, to form the Southern Railway in 1923. Under the direction of its visionary General Manager, Herbert Walker, the Southern decided to standardise on the direct current third rail as a means of current collection, rather than the overhead AC system favoured by the Brighton company, and this decision enabled it to extend electrification rapidly and at relatively low cost.

The suburban area was largely complete by 1930, and attention was then turned to the longer-distance routes to the coast, with that to Brighton and Worthing becoming Britain's first electrified main line in 1932. This was quickly followed by extensions to Eastbourne and Hastings in 1935, Portsmouth via Guildford in 1937, and Portsmouth via Horsham and Chichester in 1938. There were also some shorter 'inland' extensions, to Sevenoaks in 1935, and to Reading, Gillingham and Maidstone in 1939 before the Second World War put a stop to further development.

Little happened during the immediate post-war period of austerity and recovery, but in 1955 the now state-owned British Railways unveiled its Modernisation Plan. This presaged the eventual removal of steam traction across the network, to be replaced by new diesel locomotives and large-scale electrification schemes, although it was left to individual regions to make the case for one system or the other within their areas. All future main-line electrification would use the 25kv AC overhead system, the only exception to this policy being extension of existing electrified networks around London.

Electrification of the lines to the Kent coast and Channel ports, originally envisaged in the Southern Railway's 1946 electrification plan, was specifically provided for in the Modernisation Plan. It counted as one of the 'extensions' referred to above, and marked a continuation of the tried and tested third rail system. It was implemented in two stages between 1959 and 1962. However, when attention was turned next to the Weymouth route, the original plan was that it would be electrified on the overhead system, and would include the lines between Basingstoke and Salisbury, together with the diversionary route from Clapham Junction to Byfleet Junction via Richmond, Feltham and Chertsey. As planning progressed, though, the complexity of installing catenary in the congested suburban area, together with increasing pressure on budgets, led to a rethink.

The overhead system was not completely out of the picture initially, and as late as May 1963, costings of £28.5 million were submitted for extension of the third rail from Brookwood to Basingstoke, with 25kV catenary continuing westwards from there. Consideration was also given to the use of a side-contact third rail operating at 1,500 volts DC. This was attractive, partly because such a system is less susceptible to disruption from ice and snow, and also because the higher voltage allows the distance between substations to be increased. However, as with the overhead system, it came with the same interoperability problems of non-standard rolling stock, which eliminated any cost savings arising from the reduced number of substations.

In the end, both systems were rejected in favour of the Southern's standard third-rail system, and further cost savings were found by reducing the area to be electrified to just 90 route miles, with Basingstoke to Salisbury and Bournemouth to Weymouth dropped from the plan. In addition, the final scheme only 'washed its face' financially because the first 30 miles or so of the route already had third rail installed, and because the accompanying resignalling was excluded from the budget, the existing equipment being life-expired and due for renewal in any case. Despite these cutbacks, the summer of 1967 finally saw the introduction of regular electric services to Bournemouth, eliminating the last main-line steam workings in Britain.

While a number of smaller extensions and 'infill' projects were completed in later years – Sanderstead to East Grinstead, Tonbridge to Hastings, and Bournemouth to Weymouth in the 1980s, with Portsmouth to Southampton and Redhill to Tonbridge following during the next decade – the Bournemouth scheme remains the last main-line electrification project carried out using the third-rail system.

It now seems unlikely that any further third-rail electrification will be carried out, and that the AC overhead system will be used for all future extensions, even within the current third-rail area. Consideration has even been given to converting existing third-rail routes to the overhead system, although there are no firm proposals for this at the time of writing.

With a little over fifty years having now passed since this last main-line third-rail electrification, and with little possibility of any future installations, it seems an appropriate time to look back over the last five decades of electric trains to Bournemouth, and to consider what the future might hold.

1
Overview

The end of steam. On Sunday 9 July 1967, the day before the start of the full electric timetable, 'Merchant Navy' class 35030, *Elder Dempster Lines*, awaits departure from Southampton Central with the 14.07 Weymouth to Waterloo service, the very last steam-hauled passenger service on the Bournemouth line. Suitable inscriptions have been chalked on the smokebox door! *John H Bird/ANISTR.COM*

The revised Bournemouth electrification scheme was submitted to the BR board for approval in 1963, and this was granted the following year, the total cost now being around £15 million (around £300 million at 2018 prices). This important route served a number of destinations with diverse customer requirements: London commuters, predominantly from Winchester inwards but also from points further west; Southampton Docks with its ocean liners and significant freight traffic; day-trippers and holiday travellers to Bournemouth and other Dorset resorts, and finally Weymouth, another holiday destination, but also the departure point for ferry services to the Channel Islands. In addition, there were two branch lines off the main route; to Lymington, with its ferry services to Yarmouth on the Isle of Wight, and to Swanage, a seaside destination on the Isle of Purbeck. It was estimated that electrification would result in increased revenues of £1.1 million and reduced operating costs of £1.3 million – a net improvement of £2.4 million, even before allowing for potential traffic increases arising from expansion in areas such as Southampton, Basingstoke and Farnborough.

Of all of the Southern's routes, this one was arguably the most 'main line' in character – a superbly aligned and gently graded four-track route for almost 45 miles from Clapham Junction to west of Basingstoke, with the largely double track 30 miles onwards to Southampton equally suitable for high-speed running. The transit of that city and its suburbs imposed some restrictions, but the 25 miles or so through the New Forest and on to Bournemouth also provided some opportunities for fast running. While, at 108 miles, Bournemouth would be the

Overview

Approval for the Bournemouth electrification was granted in 1964, and the November edition of *Modern Railways* magazine of that year carried a detailed article describing the scheme. *Kevin Robertson Collection*

Front cover of the South Western Division timetable effective from Monday, 10 July. The new Bournemouth electric service was set out in Table 46. *Author's collection*

furthest destination from London served by the third rail, the first 30 miles or so of the route out of London was already electrified as a result of earlier schemes.

Electric trains had first reached as far west as Pirbright Junction on the main line under the Southern Railway Portsmouth and Alton scheme of 1937. There was a further short extension to Sturt Lane Junction, near Farnborough, to connect with the Ascot to Aldershot spur of the Reading electrification in 1939. The 1967 scheme therefore entailed electrification west from these points, through Basingstoke, Winchester, Southampton and the New Forest to Branksome, the first station beyond Bournemouth. This short extension was necessary to allow electric trains access to a new depot at Bournemouth, where they would be stabled and serviced. The third rail was also installed over the short branch line from Brockenhurst to Lymington Pier.

Colour-light signalling was installed over much of the route, but semaphore signalling remained initially between Hampton Court Junction and Woking, in the St Denys and Southampton areas, and around Brockenhurst, Lymington Junction and Christchurch. It would be some years before all of these remaining 'pockets', were resignalled. Between Woking and Basingstoke, the new signalling replaced one of the longest sections of automatic semaphore signalling in Britain, installed by the London and South Western Railway between 1902 and 1904.

Rolling stock proved to be one of the most challenging aspects of the project. All of the Southern's earlier electrification schemes had seen most passenger services operated by electric multiple-units (EMU), in which each train set or 'unit' had its own traction motors, and so could operate on its own, or coupled in multiple with other units to form a longer train. However, the particular requirements of this route meant that a rather more complex solution was required. Although the third rail would end at Branksome, the new service pattern would still require trains to run through to Weymouth from Waterloo. One option considered was locomotive haulage for all services, with a change from electric to diesel traction at Bournemouth. However, platform lengths at Waterloo would have limited train length, given the requirement to accommodate both the inbound locomotive, and that attaching at the 'country' end to take the train out again. In addition, operating diagrams meant that most stock would have to berth overnight at Bournemouth, giving little opportunity for the locomotives to be deployed elsewhere

The first of the 4-REP 'tractor' units, 3001, poses for an official publicity shot on 7 March 1967. *British Rail*

when not employed on passenger workings. So instead, an ingenious variation of the EMU concept using 'tractor' and 'trailer control' units was developed.

The new stock comprised a number of high-powered four-car tractor units (designated 4-REP under the Southern's multiple-unit coding system), and a rather larger number of unpowered three- and four-car trailer control units (3- and 4-TC), these latter having driving cabs and full multiple-unit control equipment, but no traction motors. A typical down train from Waterloo comprised a 4-REP (at the buffer-stop end) propelling one or two 4-TCs. The REP had eight traction motors totalling 3,200hp – slightly more than the output of three conventional four-car units – while the driver controlled the whole formation from the cab in the leading TC unit.

On arrival at Bournemouth, one or both of the TC units were coupled to a multiple working-equipped Class 33/1 diesel-electric locomotive, which hauled them on to Weymouth. For the return trip, the locomotive propelled the TCs back to Bournemouth – controlled from the leading cab – where they were coupled up to another REP that hauled them back to Waterloo. With a planned maximum speed of 90mph over much of the route between Bournemouth and London, this represented the first use of push-pull trains running at high speeds in the UK, and pre-dated by many years the later operations between Edinburgh and Glasgow, and on the East and West Coast main lines. However, it was only permitted by the (then) Ministry of Transport after extensive testing – much of it carried out on the main lines in Kent using various combinations of locomotives, hauled coaching stock, and multiple-units with the motors isolated – had established that there were no safety issues.

For stopping services, which would not venture over the non-electrified section west of Branksome, a new class of four-car EMU (4-VEP) was introduced. The first twenty of these were allocated to the Bournemouth line, but the class proved itself so useful that over the following seven years a total of 194 were built, and these were widely used throughout the Southern Region.

In addition to services beyond Bournemouth, locomotive haulage was also required throughout from London for the Channel Islands boat trains to Weymouth Quay, the 'Ocean Liner' expresses to Southampton, together with freight, mail and newspaper traffic. The Southern already had a growing fleet of Class 73 electro-diesels, but something rather more powerful was required to handle these heavy trains over the electrified section in the same sort of timings as the REP/TC formations. A solution was found by converting ten Class 71 electric locomotives – originally built for the Kent Coast scheme but now surplus to requirements – into Class 74 electro-diesels, with the diesel generators allowing them to make their way into Southampton Docks 'off the juice'.

The initial Bournemouth electric timetable was based around the familiar Southern fixed interval structure, with the usual mix of fast, semi-fast and stopping services. A fast service (headcode '91') left Waterloo every 2 hours, calling at Southampton Central (79 miles in 70 minutes), Bournemouth (108 miles in 100 minutes), and principal stations to Weymouth. An hourly semi-fast service ('92') called at Woking, Basingstoke, Winchester, Eastleigh, Southampton Airport (then newly opened), Southampton Central and principal stations on to Bournemouth. On alternate hours, when the fast service did not run, the semi-fast continued on from Bournemouth calling at all stations to Weymouth, thus providing it with a broadly hourly service.

An hourly stopping service ('93') called at Surbiton, Woking, and all stations except Southampton Airport to Bournemouth, taking a lengthy 174 minutes to complete the journey. This was supplemented on alternate half hours with a service to Basingstoke, making the same stops. The Lymington branch was normally served by an hourly shuttle service from Brockenhurst, connecting there with the semi-fast services, but there were some through trains to and from Waterloo at weekends. Similar arrangements operated over the other coastal branch from Wareham to Swanage, although this was beyond the range of the electrified area.

The fast and semi-fast services were normally worked by REP/TC combinations as far as Bournemouth, with Class 33/1 locomotives working the TCs beyond. Stopping services were usually in the hands of the new 4-VEPs and existing 2-HAP units, while a single 2-HAP generally sufficed for the Lymington shuttles. The Swanage branch was served by a Class 205 diesel electric multiple-unit (DEMU), except for through services to London which made use of Class 33/1 and TC combinations.

This, then, gives a 'snapshot' of the position immediately following electrification in 1967. The fifty years since then have seen many changes, including timetable recasts, further resignalling, electrification on to Weymouth along with the missing South Hampshire 'gaps', and two generations of new rolling stock. Weymouth now has two trains an hour from London, Bournemouth three, and Winchester four, and all services are in the hands of modern air-conditioned rolling stock. In the chapters that follow, we shall look back at the original implementation of the scheme, and at all that has happened since.

2
Track, Signalling, Electrification and Other Works

Work on the scheme started in 1965, and involved reballasting and relaying the fast lines with continuous welded rails (CWR) between London and Worting Junction, west of Basingstoke, together with the double track section beyond. Realignment was carried out where necessary to allow for a maximum speed of 90mph.

Flat-bottomed rails of 110lb per yard were transported to the site initially in lengths of 300ft, later increased to 600ft. On site, they were mounted on resilient pads on concrete sleepers, secured with 'Pandrol' steel clips, and welded continuously, one rail being insulated to allow track-circuiting. Although the Southern had its own equipment, additional capacity was provided by the loan of a mobile welding unit from London Transport, which was stored – when not in use – in the former Stoneham sidings south of Eastleigh.

Local freight facilities had been withdrawn at many stations, leaving goods yards and sidings redundant and, in many cases, subsequently turned over to car parking space.

Rationalisation of track layouts was therefore carried out at various locations, with the removal of points and crossings no longer required. Other alterations were also made to suit new operating requirements, notably:

The provision of four electrified berthing sidings at Basingstoke;

the upgrading of the former down goods loop from Shawford Junction around the back of Shawford station for use by passenger trains, and the provision of an additional platform facing on to it;

Above: **Track relaying work in progress on the down fast line at Barton Mill, east of Basingstoke, in late 1965. The concrete sleepers have already been laid, with temporary jointed rails, on the new ballast. The temporary rails are then removed and replaced with long welded lengths, as seen in this view.** *Tony Woodforth/Kevin Robertson Collection*

Opposite: **Track relaying in progress alongside platform 3 at Basingstoke in late 1965.** *Tony Woodforth/Kevin Robertson Collection*

removal of the up and down middle lines through the station at Bournemouth, and the provision of two berthing sidings at the west end, one capable of accommodating a locomotive and twelve coaches, and the other for a locomotive and eight coaches. The up and down platform lines were resignalled for reversible working;

the removal of all sidings and points at Lymington Town and Lymington Pier.

Relaying of the fast lines between Brookwood and Basingstoke was carried out in a number of stages during 1965 – Brookwood to Farnborough between early June and 15 August, Farnborough to Winchfield from 16 August to 10 October, Winchfield to Hook from 11 October to 7 November, and Hook to Basingstoke from 8 November to 12 December. All services used the slow lines during this period, with journey times to and from Bournemouth extended by about 15 minutes. Trains could run at line speed on the slow lines, except when passing the work sites, where a 30mph restriction applied.

On the largely double track section on to Southampton, work was carried out during weekend possessions, with services diverted either over the Mid-Hants line via Alton, or via Guildford and Havant. West of Southampton, where no diversionary route existed, single-line working was instituted over a number of stretches to allow relaying of the adjacent line and installation of conductor rails. This was the case, for example, between Brockenhurst and Beaulieu Road for two months from 3 October, resulting in delays of 10 to 20 minutes, and for six weeks from 2 January 1966 between New Milton and Hinton Admiral, with 10-minute delays.

As part of the publicity campaign surrounding the scheme, 200 invited season ticket holders were given the opportunity to view the work in progress from an engineers' inspection saloon, borrowed from the Eastern Region. This was attached to the rear of the 07.24 Bournemouth to Waterloo and 16.35 return working on dates between 23 August and 8 September. Twelve of the invited guests were carried at a time, seated in individual armchairs, and served coffee on the London-bound trip, and tea on the return.

Signalling

As mentioned earlier, the main signalling works comprised the installation of continuous colour-light signalling from Woking (where the station area had previously been resignalled as part of the Portsmouth scheme in 1937) to St Denys, together with shorter stretches between Northam Junction and Southampton Central, Totton and Brockenhurst, Lymington Junction and Christchurch, and Pokesdown and Branksome. The Woking to St Denys section used mainly three-aspect signals, with some four-aspects in areas where signals were more closely spaced, notably around Farnborough, Winchfield, Basingstoke and Eastleigh. Two-aspect signals were used between Totton and Brockenhurst. The new signalling allowed fast trains to run at headways of 3 minutes, and stopping services at 3 to 5 minutes.

New power signal boxes were opened at Basingstoke and Eastleigh, equipped with 'entrance exit' route setting panels and digital train describers. These buildings were to the 'CLASP' design (an acronym for Consortium Local Authority Special Programme), constructed largely from concrete prefabricated

Signalling changes in progress at Basingstoke, 1966. The new power signal box nears completion while semaphores and the old Basingstoke 'A' box remain in charge for the time being. *Tony Woodforth/Kevin Robertson Collection*

A fine gantry of LSWR lower quadrant automatic semaphores at Fleet, with replacement colour-lights awaiting commissioning in front. Interestingly, the semaphores saw sixty-four years' service from 1902 to 1966, while the colour-lights gave way to still newer equipment in 2010, just forty-four years later. *Tony Woodforth/Kevin Robertson Collection*

Further signalling progress. In this 1966 view at Basingstoke, part of the new 'entrance-exit' (NX) panel is lifted ready for installation in the signal box. *Kevin Robertson Collection*

The new CLASP buildings under construction on the down side island at Eastleigh. A Class 33/0 diesel-electric locomotive passes on the down fast line with a train of 'Presflo' cement wagons. As can be seen, both this and the up fast line have been recently relaid, and conductor rails are in place on all lines. *John H Bird/ANISTR.COM*

Signalling in transition at Swaythling on 22 October 1967. A new colour-light awaits commissioning, mounted temporarily at an angle so as not to obstruct sighting of the existing semaphore. *John H Bird/ANISTR.COM*

panels on a steel frame, similar to a number of station buildings that began to appear around the same time. The design had been used previously at Guildford in 1965, and was later used for the new box at Portsmouth and Southsea in 1968.

The new box at Eastleigh controlled the section from St Denys to just west of Worting Junction, while from there to Farnborough came under the supervision of Basingstoke. Additional panels installed in the 1937 power box at Woking controlled the eastern end of the area, including the connection to the Alton line at Pirbright Junction. Elsewhere, new signalling was controlled from existing manual signal boxes, while semaphore signalling – with some modifications – remained in use between Hampton Court Junction and Woking, St Denys and Totton, Brockenhurst to Lymington Junction, and Christchurch to Pokesdown. The single-track Lymington branch was worked on the 'one engine in steam' system beyond Lymington Junction, and the signal boxes at Lymington Town and Pier reduced in status to ground frames to work their respective level crossings. Winchester Junction box was also retained to work the connection with the Mid Hants line to Alton, including the token exchange arrangements, but its signals were electrically released from Eastleigh.

The new signalling was commissioned in various stages between June 1966 and February 1967 as below, resulting in the closure of thirty mechanical signal boxes:

- 5 June 1966 – Woking to Farnborough and Ash Vale (on the line to Alton);
- 7 September 1966 – Eastleigh to St Denys (down line only);
- 2 October 1966 – Northam Junction to Southampton Central;
- 23 October 1966 – Totton to Brockenhurst;
- 30 October 1966 – Farnborough to Basingstoke;
- 6 November 1966 – Winchester to St Denys, Eastleigh to Botley and Chandlers Ford (on the lines to Fareham and Romsey respectively);
- 13 November 1966 – Winchester to Wootton (south of Worting Junction);
- 20 November 1966 – Basingstoke to Wootton, also to Bramley and Overton (on the lines to Reading and Salisbury respectively);
- 11 December 1966 – Pokesdown to Bournemouth;
- 15 January 1967 – Bournemouth to Branksome;
- 26 February 1967 – Lymington Junction to Christchurch.

Electrification

Electrification works involved the installation of conductor rail on the fast lines between Woking and Sturt Lane Junction (the slow lines having been dealt with under the pre-war Reading scheme), and on all lines west of there to Branksome. This included the long loops at Wallers Ash, between Micheldever and Winchester, and the whole of the Lymington branch. Conductor rail was also installed from Branksome into Bournemouth depot, and in carriage sidings at a number of locations.

Conductor rails with a weight of 106lb per yard were used for most of the scheme, but a heavier version – at 150lb per yard – was used through Southampton Tunnel and on the whole of the Lymington branch. The rails were welded into 300ft lengths before being transported to the site, and then welded together in situ to give maximum lengths of 1,530ft between expansion gaps.

Electrification work is in evidence during 1965 at Lyndhurst Road, in the New Forest, as a Class 33/0 diesel-electric locomotive passes with a service from Waterloo to Bournemouth West. Conductor rails are in place on the up line, while insulator 'pots' have been installed on the down.
Christopher J Wilson Collection

Power was taken from the National Grid at Basingstoke, Southampton and Bournemouth, and then distributed at 33 kilovolts to nineteen substations with intermediate track paralleling huts. These were located at Fleet, Winchfield, Newnham, Barton, Worting Junction, Waltham, Northbrook, Kings Worthy (located on the site of the former junction to Worthy Down), Shawford, Eastleigh, Southampton, Totton, Ashurst, Woodfidley, Lymington Junction, New Milton, Hinton Admiral, Pokesdown and Bournemouth. In addition to a stretch of the main line, the substation at Lymington Junction also fed the whole of the branch to Lymington Pier.

Each substation contained a transformer to bring the voltage down to 750v to be fed to the live rail, and either one or two rectifiers to convert the alternating current to direct current. The five new substations from Fleet to Worting Junction each contained a single 2 megawatt rectifier, while twelve of the remainder on to Bournemouth each had two 1MW rectifiers. The substations at Eastleigh and Bournemouth each contained two rectifiers having a higher rating of 1.5MW. Newer technology, specifically the use of track current relays, allowed the distance between the substations west of Worting Junction to be increased to almost 4.5 miles, against the 3.5-mile spacing common on earlier schemes. This allowed an overall saving of four substations and three track paralleling huts.

The purpose of the track paralleling huts was primarily to reduce the voltage drop between the substations either side, by the use of parallel connections to the conductor rail sections fed by those substations. They were also equipped with circuit breakers, allowing the isolation of a substation in the event of a fault. Control of the network was shared between the existing control room at Woking (covering the Fleet to Winchester section), and a new facility housed in a 100ft-long brick building at Eastleigh (Winchester to Bournemouth). This substantial structure also contained a telephone exchange, workshops, store rooms, offices, mess rooms and other staff facilities.

The substations and track paralleling huts were built to a new design, which had first been tried experimentally at Hollingbourne in 1962 as part of the Kent Coast electrification. The electrical equipment was housed inside rectangular prefabricated buildings of aluminium alloy. Mostly painted light grey, they could hardly be described as attractive, but a small concession was made to their surroundings by applying green paint to those in the New Forest, between Totton and Christchurch!

Power was switched on to the live rail in stages, as set out below:

12 December 1966 – Pirbright Junction to Northbrook substation (south of Micheldever), together with the four carriage sidings at Barton Mill, Basingstoke;

14 December 1966 – Northbrook substation to Swaythling;

18 January 1967 – Swaythling to Lymington Junction.

6 March 1967 – Lymington Junction to Bournemouth;

28 March 1967 – Bournemouth to Branksome and Bournemouth depot

8 May 1967 – Lymington Junction to Lymington Pier.

Each of these extensions was preceded by a run with a special locomotive-hauled test train including a multiple-unit driving vehicle, with engineers travelling in an adjacent brake van carefully checking the alignment and height of the live rail.

Single-line working between Sway and New Milton on 31 October 1966. The picture was taken from the 16.02 Eastleigh to Bournemouth service, running 'wrong line' along the up line, while work takes place on the down. *John H Bird/ANISTR.COM*

Track, Signalling, Electrification and Other Works

Track remodelling in progress at Bournemouth, seen from the signal box on 27 November 1966. The centre roads have been removed, and connections for the new berthing sidings at the west end are being laid in. *Peter Pescod/Transport Treasury*

A further view of change under way at Bournemouth, this time from the east end, with the centre roads removed, new colour-light signals in operation, but conductor rails yet to be laid. The picture is undated, but must be late 1966 or early 1967. A fascinating test formation is leaving the up platform, comprising Class 33/1 diesel-electric locomotive D6521 sandwiched between a pair of 4-TC units, with 419 at the rear. It was not unknown for this to happen later in passenger service, causing much confusion for those waiting to board! *A D McIntyre*

Conductor rail alignment checks in progress near Millbrook on 6 January 1967. Class 73 electro-diesel locomotive E6043 hauls a brake van and a motor coach from former 6-PAN unit 3031. *John H Bird/ANISTR.COM*

Other Works

A new maintenance depot with berthing sidings was built on the route to the former Bournemouth West terminus, which was closed in October 1965. This line was originally accessed via a triangular junction east of Branksome station, but the viaduct carrying the eastern chord was in poor condition and repairs were ruled out on cost grounds (although it still stands, trackless, more than half a century later!). Access therefore was only possible via the western chord, hence the extension of the live rail to Branksome, and the need for trains to reverse there to enter or leave the depot.

As well as maintaining the electric multiple-units and locomotives based at Bournemouth, the depot would also carry out servicing of inter-regional trains, refuelling of main line diesel locomotives, and maintenance of diesel shunting locomotives employed at Bournemouth and Weymouth.

The main depot building was 295ft long, steel-framed and clad in asbestos sheeting with panels of translucent polyester resin on both the sides and roof, to admit as much natural light as possible. The building was fully heated to provide a comfortable working environment for staff, and all the rail entrances had electrically operated roller shutter doors. Inside the building were four tracks with inspection pits, each 283ft long to accommodate a four-car multiple-unit. Equipment included a 5-ton overhead travelling crane working in conjunction with four 15-ton mobile electric lifting jacks, to facilitate the removal and installation of wheelsets and traction motors. For safety reasons, the conductor rails terminated on all four roads outside the depot entrances at both ends, but overhead cables were provided inside, and multiple-units could collect power from these via temporary trolley equipment.

Further berthing facilities were provided at Eastleigh, in the form of new sidings to accommodate four twelve-coach trains, and enlargement of the existing diesel multiple-unit shed to provide eight tracks with a capacity of thirty-two coaches. Space for these facilities was freed up with the demolition of the steam shed.

Station improvements were extensive, primarily involving the lengthening of platforms to accommodate twelve-coach trains at Brookwood, Farnborough, Fleet, Basingstoke, Winchester, Eastleigh and Bournemouth. Disused central platforms facing on to the fast lines were removed at Farnborough, Winchfield and Hook, while the opposite took place at Micheldever, where the loops and side platforms were removed, and the central island platform reinstated between the two remaining lines. At Fleet, the station building was replaced with a new structure to the 'CLASP' design, while a similar – but larger – replacement was provided for the downside buildings at Eastleigh.

Platform extension in progress at Farnborough in 1965. The new prefabricated concrete sections are in place on the up side, but cannot be connected to the existing platform until the semaphore gantry has been removed. At this early date, the fast lines have still to be relaid, although the connection from the sidings to the down slow line has been severed, just ahead of 'West Country' class, 34089, which is passing with a down service.
Norman Simmons/Kevin Robertson Collection

A brand new but fairly basic station, comprising concrete platforms linked by a footbridge, with a waiting shelter on the up side, was built to serve Southampton Airport, just south of Eastleigh. This opened on 18 April 1966.

Southampton Terminus and Northam Station, situated on the eastern side of the Northam Junction triangle, were closed on 5 September 1966, although the line into the docks was retained for use by boat trains.

At Southampton Central the original up side buildings, which dated from 1892 and included a clock tower, were demolished to make way for a new structure comprising ticket office, waiting room, toilets and staff accommodation at platform level, with four floors of office space above at the London end, added subsequently.

The existing subway at Bournemouth was replaced by a new footbridge, but the overall roof was retained.

More generally, Southern Region green signage was replaced by the new British Rail corporate style, with clear black 'Rail Alphabet' script on a white background. Three major stations had their names shortened – Winchester City, Southampton Central and Bournemouth Central becoming, respectively, Winchester, Southampton and Bournemouth.

On 15 March 1967, Class 33 diesel-electric locomotive D6520 propels a 4-TC unit out of Southampton Central with a London-bound service. Behind, the old up side buildings with their clock tower have been demolished, and work has started on construction of the new ticket office and the four-storey office block. *John H Bird/ANISTR.COM*

The new – and fairly basic – Southampton Airport station, opened on 18 April 1966, and is seen here in the summer of that year. Conductor rail has yet to be laid on the down line, although the insulators are in place, and a post for a new colour-light signal has been installed behind the semaphore distant. A down train passes behind an unidentified locomotive. *Kevin Robertson Collection*

One of the new substations, at Fleet, showing the grey-painted aluminium alloy construction – functional, but hardly a triumph of aesthetics! *Kevin Robertson Collection*

The new layout at Micheldever, 18 March 1967. The platform loops have been lifted, and the previously disused island platform brought back into use to serve the former fast lines only. Later, the down platform and buildings, seen here, would also be removed, although those on the up side remain to this day, linked to the island by a subway. 'Merchant Navy' Class 35013 passes with the 13.30 Waterloo to Weymouth service. *John H Bird/ANISTR.COM*

Signs of change at Shawford Junction, south of Winchester, on 18 March 1967. The new substation can be seen on the left, alongside the formation of the former Didcot, Newbury and Southampton railway. A new facing connection has been provided from the down main line to the down loop. Class 73 electro-diesel locomotive E6012 propels a southbound test train formed of two 4-TC units, both in three-car formation awaiting delivery of their trailer first vehicles. *John H Bird/ANISTR.COM*

3
Rolling Stock

The EMU stock provided for the Bournemouth scheme comprised thirty-one 3- and 4-TC (**T**railer **C**ontrol) units, eleven 4-REP (**R**estaurant **E**lectro **P**neumatic tractor) units, and twenty 4-VEP (**V**estibule **E**lectro **P**neumatic) units. The tractor and trailer concept to facilitate through working to Weymouth has already been mentioned, but this was not the only way in which this scheme differed from earlier ones. Much of this stock was not new at all, but instead comprised refurbished locomotive hauled Mark 1 coaches surplus to requirements elsewhere, in some cases – ironically – because of the introduction of new Mark 2 coaches! This approach was driven largely by the scheme's budgetary constraints, but also because of the limited capacity of BR's workshops at the time, which would have struggled to produce the required number of new vehicles in the timescales required.

Starting with the TC units, these were formed entirely by 'recycling' existing stock. The unit formation was Driving Trailer Second Open (DTSO), Trailer Brake Second Corridor (TBSK), Trailer First Corridor (TFK), and a further DTSO; in the 3-TC units the TFK was omitted. There were twenty-eight four-car units and three three-car units. The latter were generally used – with a pair of four-car units – to make up eleven-coach trains for push-pull working with a Class 73 locomotive, such formations being used to provide additional capacity in the peak periods.

A Waterloo to Weymouth service is caught by the camera west of Lymington Junction, formed of a pair of 4-TC units propelled by a Class 33 locomotive, unit 419 leading. The picture is undated, but the diesel traction suggests it is before the start of full electric working.
Kevin Robertson Collection

On 9 May 1967, a couple of months before the start of the full electric timetable, a Waterloo to Bournemouth service comprising a pair of 4-TC units propelled by a 4-REP – what was to become the 'standard' formation on the route – calls at Winchester. One of the aluminium-clad track paralleling huts is visible at the far end of the up platform. *britishrailwayphotographs.com/John A M Vaughan*

The scenic New Forest location of Lyndhurst Road Station - still complete with telegraph poles – provides the setting for a Weymouth to Waterloo service in the early days of electric working. Unusually, the 4-TC units – 408 and 410 – were at the front and rear of the train, with an unidentified 4-REP providing power in the centre. *britishrailwayphotographs.com/John A M Vaughan*

Above: **On 11 April 1968, 4-TC unit no 403 leads the 12.56 Bournemouth to Waterloo service past Pokesdown. At this date the through roads, semaphores and signal box had another four years or so to go before rationalisation and resignalling would sweep them away.** *John Scrace*

Left: **Driving cab of one of the new Bournemouth units – this is a 4-TC, but REPs and VEPs were near identical, as were other contemporary SR units. The brake controller is on the left, with the master controller on the right. The 'loudaphone' intercom to communicate with the guard is upper left, with the AWS indicator below, while the gauges in front of the driver are, from left to right, master reservoir/brake pipe pressure, brake cylinder pressure, and speedometer.** *John H Bird/ANISTR.COM*

The DTSO vehicles were formed from former Tourist Second Open (TSO) coaches, whose original layout comprised two saloons each containing four eight-seat bays, providing sixty-four seats in total. There were three transverse entrance vestibules, one at each end of the seating area, and one between the two saloons. At one end, between the vestibule and the vehicle end, were two toilets. The conversion work involved the removal of these toilets and their replacement by a driving cab with standard multiple-unit controls, together with the fitting of the Southern's '1963 stock' gangwayed front end formed from moulded glass-reinforced plastic (GRP) with steel framing. The entrance vestibule behind the cab became the driver's dedicated entrance, with inward opening doors, so in order to retain adequate passenger access, external doors were let into the first seating bay, with the former large window replaced by narrow 'quarter lights' either side of the door. Internally, the vehicles were finished in the latest Southern multiple-unit style, similar to the contemporary CIG and BIG units, with Formica panelling and new blue and green check seat moquette. In terms of running and electrical gear, vehicles were fitted with coil-sprung B5(S) bogies, electro-pneumatic (EP) and air brakes, and electric heating, in place of the original equipment. No pick-up shoes were carried, the electrical supply being provided by a motor generator fed by the train heating supply from the 4-REP unit or a locomotive, and all of the Bournemouth units carried the standard train heating jumper cables and sockets for this purpose. As a result, there was very little underframe equipment compared with conventional multiple-unit stock, and these vehicles weighed in at 32 tons.

Second-class compartment in a 4-TC unit. As with the open vehicles, the accommodation was spacious enough, but hardly the height of luxury! *BR*

First-class compartment in a 4-TC unit. In exchange for a more expensive ticket, you got a bit more legroom and width with the three-aside seating, a limited reclining facility, an antimacassar and an umbrella rack. *BR*

The TBSK and TFK vehicles retained their internal layouts largely unchanged, the former providing thirty-two seats in four compartments, along with a guard's compartment, large luggage/parcels cage, and a toilet. The guard's compartment, however, was reduced in size from the fairly large space provided in the vehicle's original incarnation (which had to accommodate a large handbrake wheel on a vertical column), to the compact arrangement as found in the contemporary CIG, BIG and VEP units. As a consequence, the window originally positioned just beyond the guard's door on the compartment side was plated over, although its counterpart on the opposite side of the coach remained, to admit light to the corridor. The TFK provided forty-two first-class seats in seven compartments, and two toilets. Internal changes were limited to new panelling and moquette, as in the DTSO vehicle, although a charcoal grey check pattern was used in the first-class compartments. B5(S) bogies, EP/air brakes, and electric heating was fitted to both vehicles, while the motor generator and brake compressor were installed under the TBSK. Weights were little different from the DTSO vehicles, with the TBSK turning the scales at 35 tons, and the TFK at 33. In all of the converted vehicles, windows were replaced where necessary with the later Mark 1 external framed version, while toilet windows were to the standard SR '1963' pattern, with opaque glass and no central vent in the small upper pane.

Turning to the REP units, while the centre trailers were also refurbished former locomotive-hauled coaches, a different approach was required for the Driving Motor Second Open (DMSO) vehicles. As well as having all axles motored, a lot of heavy electrical equipment had to be carried on the underframe, and so these vehicles were built new, but to an identical layout to the DTSO in the TC units. Seating units, however, being brand new, were to a similar design to that used in the experimental 'XP64' vehicles, and on subsequent builds of 4-CIG and 4-BIG units. At around 52 tons, these vehicles were virtually electric locomotives with passenger accommodation, and indeed, below the floor they were not dissimilar to the Class 73 electro-diesels, with which they shared the same traction motors and Mark 6 bogies. Those motors, designated EE546, were rated at 400hp, giving each DMSO an output of 1,600hp, and a total for the unit of 3,200hp, an unprecedented figure for a single set at the time (and only 100hp short of the Class 55 'Deltic' locomotives operating on the East Coast main line). Although electrically compatible with most other Southern stock, the REPs rarely worked with other powered units in practice, as the combined current consumption on starting would have overloaded the electrical supply!

With such high installed power drawing very heavy currents, it was recognised that severe arcing problems might occur at conductor rails breaks, particularly in icy conditions

4-REP unit 3009 stands at Brockenhurst, wearing the original dull blue livery, with small yellow warning panel on the gangway door, and white numerals. The picture is undated and interestingly, while the unit carries the headcode '92', suggesting a normal service train, it is not accompanied by TC units.
Kevin Robertson Collection

4-REP unit 3010 leads a Weymouth to Waterloo service through the New Forest during 1968. The REPs were usually marshalled with the buffet car as the third vehicle from the London end, but this unit has been turned at some point, meaning that meal service would be made into the inner four bays of the leading DMSO. Tablecloths and menu cards can just be seen through the windows of this section. *Christopher J Wilson Collection*

where one pick-up shoe could be drawing the majority of the current. The problem was addressed by providing two separate power circuits in each unit, each feeding two of the motors in each DMS vehicle. Each circuit was fed by separate pick-up shoes, of which there were four (two per side) on each motor bogie. The effect of these arrangements was to restrict the current drawn by each pick-up shoe to no more than 2,000 amps in most circumstances.

Of the two intermediate trailers, the Trailer Buffet (TRB) was converted from a standard Mark 1 Restaurant Buffet (RB) vehicle, and the work involved was fairly extensive. As built, these vehicles had a seating area for twenty-three passengers in loose chairs around tables at one end, a small buffet counter, pantry, kitchen, staff compartment and a staff toilet, these last two compartments flanking the passage to the gangway. The seating area was left unchanged, but the buffet counter area was increased in length by removal of the pantry. The end of the bar nearest the seating area was angled, and a former staff door into the buffet area now provided external access between the bar and the seating area. In the kitchen, the cooking equipment – which included a grill, griddle plate, frying plate, deep fat fryer, four-hole egg-poacher, hot cupboard and refrigerator – was converted from bottled gas to electric operation, power being provided by a 200v motor generator mounted under the vehicle.

The staff compartment and staff toilet both became passenger toilets to ensure adequate provision, the only other toilet in the units being in the Trailer Brake First Corridor (TBFK).

Externally, some changes were made to window layout and design as well. There had originally been shallow windows serving both the kitchen and pantry, but as the latter was now behind the extended bar area, it was blocked up, leaving just a single shallow window – to the kitchen – on that side of the vehicle. The original staff compartment had a narrow window with standard sliding vents at the top. With the conversion of this compartment to a passenger toilet, a standard size toilet window was fitted instead, and both this and the corresponding window on the other side of the coach were replaced with the standard SR 1963 design as described above. Changes to the corridor side of the vehicle were minimal, being restricted to the removal of one window at the kitchen end, between the stores loading door and the toilet. Each of these vehicles was named after towns or geographical features close to the route, such as 'The Winchester' and 'The Solent', this being displayed on a 'pub sign'-style panel behind the buffet counter, in what could be seen as a reference to Bulleid's 'tavern cars'. These vehicles weighed 34 tons.

Full restaurant service was provided on many Bournemouth trains, and so these vehicles were marshalled with the kitchen next to the DMSO, in which the saloon at the inner end had tables permanently fitted for meal service. The two-plus-two seating in these DMS vehicles must have made for a slightly cramped dining experience – compared with the two-plus-one arrangement generally provided elsewhere – while the fairly lively riding of the Mark 6 motor bogie underneath cannot have helped much either! Another slightly unfortunate factor was

4-REP unit no 3011 pauses for custom at Southampton central at the head of a Weymouth to Waterloo service on 21 October 1967. The office block above the station buildings behind is progressing well. *John H Bird/ANISTR.COM*

Close-up view of a 4-REP motor bogie, showing the twin pick-up shoes, each feeding one of the unit's two separate power circuits. The Class 73 electro-diesels ran on similar bogies, although the shoegear on those was retractable. Also visible under the cab end is the electric train heating (ETH) cable – not normally a feature of SR multiple-units, it was essential on the Bournemouth stock to supply power to the 4-TC units. *David Brown*

The interior of a 4-REP buffet car, converted from a loco-hauled RB vehicle. In the foreground is the twenty-three-seat saloon, virtually unchanged from the vehicle's original incarnation. Immediately beyond the partition on the left is a small bar area, with a larger food-serving counter beyond that. This was followed by a corridor alongside the kitchen, and then two passenger toilets flanking the gangway to the next coach. In this staged publicity shot, a steward is serving passengers in the saloon. In practice, this area was generally occupied by passengers using the buffet facilities, while full meal service was made into the adjacent DMSO vehicle.
BR Southern Region

that, as the REP was normally the rear unit of an eight- or twelve-car train, passengers at the front wishing to use the buffet or restaurant facilities faced a lengthy walk. In addition, the orientation of units was such that meal service was normally made into the DMS coupled to the TC unit, so those passengers from further forward could only reach the buffet by walking through the dining area and past the kitchen!

The TBFK vehicle had to fulfil two functions – the provision of first-class accommodation and the guard's compartment and the luggage/parcels cage. There were insufficient surplus brake-first vehicles available to meet this requirement, so a more thorough conversion job was needed. The vehicles were formed from former Corridor Composite (CK) vehicles, the four first-class compartments and one toilet being retained, while the guards and luggage accommodation took the place of the three second-class compartments and the second toilet. As with all the other adapted vehicles, interior panelling and seating were renewed, B5(S) bogies, EP/air brakes and electric heating fitted, and windows modified where necessary. Vehicle weight was 35 tons.

Initial conversions of each vehicle type – DMSO, TFK and TBSK in the TC sets, and TRB and TBFK in the REPs – were carried out at Eastleigh, but the remainder were all done at

Interior of a 4-REP DMSO, with two-plus-two seating, orange window curtains, and longitudinal luggage racks. The accommodation was spacious and reasonably comfortable, but soon compared unfavourably with the air-conditioned Mark 2 vehicles entering service on other regions. In the vehicle marshalled next to the buffet car, the far saloon had tables permanently fitted for meal service. *Crécy Archive*

Newly delivered 4-VEP unit No. 7707 stands in Clapham Yard sidings. The livery is the same as the REP and TC units – dull, all over blue, slightly relieved by the cast aluminium BR double arrow logo below the cab side window. *S W Stevens-Stratten*

York, as was construction of the new DMSO vehicles for the REPs. This was a departure for the Southern, all of whose previous post-war rolling stock had been built at Eastleigh. The 'donor' Mark 1 coaches had been built at various dates between 1951 and 1960 – either by British Railways' own workshops or by contractors – so some were more than 15 years old by the time they started their new careers. Most were originally fitted with steam heating and vacuum braking, and rode on BR Mark 1 or 'Commonwealth' bogies, and the conversion work involved replacement of all these features as described above. As built, they also had side buffers and drophead buckeye couplers (mounted on a conventional drawhook). These features were retained at the outer ends of the TC DMS vehicles, but between vehicles within units, fixed buckeye couplers were fitted, and the buffers removed. In addition to the moulded GRP driving cab-ends fitted to each unit, inter-vehicle gangways had the 'bellows' covered by a neat metal shrouding, as in the contemporary CIG, BIG and VEP units. The TC units were the first to go into service, with three units deployed on the 07.15 Eastleigh to Waterloo, 09.30 Waterloo to Bournemouth, and 16.28 Bournemouth to Eastleigh services from 15 August 1966. At this early stage, the units were hauled conventionally by Class 33 locomotives, rather than operating in push-pull mode.

The twenty 4-VEP units were completely new build, the motor coaches being constructed at Derby Litchurch Lane, and the trailer vehicles at York. While retaining the standard BR Mark 1 bodyshell, they represented a complete departure from all earlier designs. Intended for main-line stopping and some semi-fast services, they were a successor to the earlier 2-HAP units and the pre-nationalisation HALs and BILs, but embodied *some* improvements over them, notably the provision of through gangways. Each unit comprised a Driving Trailer semi open Composite (DTCsoL) vehicle at each end, flanking a Trailer Second Open (TSO) and a Motor Brake Second Open (MBSO). The DTCsoL vehicles had a driving cab behind the standard 1963 stock front end, accessed by the obligatory driver only vestibule. Next came second-class accommodation for thirty-eight passengers in four bays of three-plus-two suburban-style seating, with entrance doors to each bay and transverse luggage racks above the seats. This was followed by four first-class compartments served by a side corridor – access to the corridor necessitating a bench seat for four against the bulkhead in the final second-class bay. The compartments were virtually identical in accommodation and trim to those in the REP and TC units, seating three passengers a side, but also having external entrance doors. There were two further external doors on the corridor side, and a toilet at

Less than two months before the start of full electric working, and only a couple of weeks after their introduction, 4-VEP units 7706 and 7705 head west past Millbrook on 20 May 1967. *John H Bird/ANISTR.COM*

the inner end of the vehicle. These vehicles weighed 34 tons.

The TSO coach was about as near to a suburban vehicle as one could get, seating ninety-eight passengers in ten bays identical to those in the DTCsoL. The MBSO was broadly similar, but with four bays sacrificed to provide the guard's and luggage accommodation, this being placed nearest the centre of the unit. These vehicles seated fifty-eight passengers, largely in three-plus-two bays, but with a bench seat for four against the bulkhead separating the guard's compartment from the saloon, similar to that in the DTCsoL. The TSO weighed 31 tons and the MBSO 48 tons, the traction motors and other equipment accounting for the difference.

All the trailer vehicles rode on B5(S) bogies, although these were fitted with stiffer springs than those on the REP and TC units, in anticipation of these units loading more heavily. The MBSO was mounted on Mark 6 motor bogies with each axle carrying an EE507 motor of 250hp. Most of the electrical and control equipment was mounted under this vehicle, there being little underframe equipment on the trailers, although the pick-up shoes were mounted on the outer bogies of each DTCsoL.

Reaction to the VEPs was mixed, and the derogatory remark that they were a '4-SUB with corridors' has been much quoted! The large number of external doors was a mixed blessing, giving the units enviably rapid loading and unloading qualities, but also resulting in draughts and representing a significant maintenance liability. By way of justifying the earlier observation that they were an improvement over earlier stock built for the same purpose, the following points should be considered:

Through gangways meant that all passengers had access to the toilets – a feature lacking in the earlier HAP and HAL units – and to other parts of the train when running in multiple;

The B5(S) bogies gave a much improved ride;

In second class, large windows stretched between each entrance door, giving a particularly light interior, made all the more cheerful initially by the fitting of orange window curtains between each bay.

The fairest comment that can probably be made about the VEPs is that they were entirely fit for the purpose for which they were intended, and the Southern clearly considered the design a success, as witnessed by the 194 units that were built and put into service throughout the region over the following seven years. They were, however, justifiably unpopular when diagrammed on long-distance express services, either on their own, or sometimes indiscriminately with express stock.

Externally, all of the new Bournemouth stock was finished in the then new 'British Rail' plain, unlined, eggshell finish blue livery, with small yellow warning panels on the end gangway doors. This fairly austere appearance was relieved very slightly by the BR double arrow logos, which were in the form of bright aluminium castings fitted below the driver's cab side windows.

Mention of VEPs on long-distance services brings us to a curious hybrid unit that was created in April 1968, less than a year after the start of electric services to Bournemouth. Availability of the REPs was sometimes a problem in the early days, with eight daily diagrams required from eleven units. Not only did this leave little reserve in the event of failures, but the

Roughly midway through their 170-odd-minute journeys, 4-VEP units 7705 and 7714 pass at Eastleigh with up and down stopping services between Bournemouth and Waterloo. *John H Bird/ANISTR.COM*

units were diagrammed to run around 12,000 miles per month, so had to visit Chart Leacon depot, at Ashford in Kent, for general running gear overhauls every five or six months. Some spare capacity was available by using 4-TC units working with Class 73 locomotives, but it was not possible to provide a catering service in such formations.

As a temporary measure, 4-VEP units 7739/41/42 – nominally destined to replace pre-war stock on the Central Division – were 'cannibalised' when new, and some of the vehicles used to form an eight-car unit for use mainly on semi-fast Bournemouth workings. Designated 8-VAB (**V**estibule **A**nd **B**uffet), and numbered 8001, this unit was effectively a three- and a five-car unit permanently coupled. The three-car part comprised two DTCsoL vehicles with a MBSO in between. The other part had a DTCsoL and a MBSO at each end, flanking a former locomotive-hauled RB vehicle (S1759), adapted for multiple-unit operation. The adaptations involved the removal of the vehicle's side buffers, replacement of its drop-head buckeye couplers with the fixed head version, and wiring changes for through multiple-unit working and electric heating. It retained its bottled gas cooking equipment. The MBSO coupled to the kitchen end of the RB had its doors permanently locked, with the outside handles removed, tables fitted, and its nominal three-plus-two seating used on a two plus-one-basis for meal service.

With three motor coaches producing a total of 3,000hp, the VAB had sufficient power for a twelve-car train, and it has been suggested that the intention was to use it in such a formation with a 4-TC unit. However, the lack of a suitable jumper cable on the VAB meant that it was unable to provide power to a TC for lighting, heating and control purposes, and such workings never actually took place. It did, however, work on occasions in a twelve-car formation with another 4-VEP unit.

In its early days, the VAB had quite a distinctive appearance, the VEP vehicles wearing the original all-over blue livery, while the RB was in blue/grey. The plain blue lasted until February 1972, when the VEP vehicles were repainted in the two-tone scheme, giving the unit a more consistent look. No. 8001 lasted in service on the Bournemouth line until 1975, by which time a further four REP units had been delivered. The VEP vehicles were then re-formed into the originally planned units (although 7739 was placed in storage), while the RB, being unsuitable for further hauled use because of the extensive modifications made, was scrapped.

On the locomotive front, central to operation of the new services were the Class 33/1 diesel-electric locomotives, which were to work the TC units over the non-electrified section to Weymouth. These were adapted from the standard Class 33 (BRCW Type 3, prior to TOPS reclassification), of which the

4-VEP unit 7715 makes its way through the New Forest with a Bournemouth to Waterloo stopping service during 1968. Christopher J Wilson Collection

Southern had a fleet of ninety-seven built by the Birmingham Railway Carriage and Wagon Company between 1960 and 1962. These were versatile mixed traffic machines powered by a Sulzer 8DLA28 diesel engine of 1,550bhp, with the DC generator feeding four 305hp traction motors in a Bo-Bo wheel arrangement. The generator and traction motors were supplied by Crompton Parkinson, giving rise to the class' popular nickname of 'Cromptons'.

Prior to the adaptations, extensive testing was carried out with locomotive D6580, which was converted to operate in push-pull mode with a six-coach set of former Southern Railway coaching stock, classified 6-TC and numbered 601. The conversion work comprised the fitting of EMU type high-level jumper connections and multiple-unit control gear, such that the locomotive's traction motors, braking, etc, could be fully controlled from the driving cab of an EMU, while an EMU could be similarly controlled from the locomotive. Interestingly, consideration was also given to allowing the locomotive's motors to draw power direct from the live rail, as it was fitted with pick-up shoes for a short time, but this idea was not pursued.

The tests proved successful, and it was decided to convert a further eighteen locomotives, the selection made on the basis of examples due for major overhaul. The locomotives chosen were D6511/13/14/16/17/19–21/25/27–29/31–33/35/36/38.

The adaptations were the same as those carried out on D6580, but included additionally the fitting of drophead buckeye couplers and Pullman rubbing plates (also fitted subsequently to D6580), which made the physical process of attaching and detaching TC units at Bournemouth much quicker and easier. On the systems side, the locomotives were completely compatible with any Southern EMU stock introduced from 1951 onwards, as well as the Class 73 and 74 locomotives described below. These locomotives easily handled a single TC unit over the Bournemouth to Weymouth section, but had to work harder on occasions when two TCs were used, especially on the steep climb from Weymouth to Bincombe Tunnel. Both they and their unadapted – but otherwise similar – Class 33/0 sisters also worked heavy Channel Islands boat trains through to Weymouth Quay.

The Class 73 electro-diesels were particularly versatile machines. They were essentially 'straight' electric locomotives drawing current from the live rail, and powered by four 400hp traction motors, two per bogie in a Bo-Bo wheel arrangement, giving a total output of 1,600hp. The clever part was the inclusion of a 600hp English Electric 4 SRKT diesel engine driving a type 824/30 generator from the same manufacturer, which enabled the locomotives to run, albeit at reduced power, over non-electrified lines. This equipment was already

First-class compartment in a 4-VEP unit. This is very similar to those in the REPs and TCs, the main difference being the external door in addition to access via the side corridor. *Crécy Archive*

in use in the Southern's various classes of DEMU, and so was safely tried and tested technology. Non-electrified routes often had insufficient clearance at the lineside for pick-up shoes, so those on the Class 73s were retractable, being lowered by compressed air from the locomotive's own compressor, or by a footpump operated by the driver, and raised by spring pressure, so 'failsafe' in the event of any air failure.

The locomotives had spacious driving cabs, with large windscreens either side of a standard Southern two-character headcode box. Controls were duplicated, allowing operation from either side of the cab. The diesel generator was mounted at one end of the locomotive, with the lighter electrical equipment at the other. What would otherwise have been an uneven weight distribution was addressed by adding 'ballast' at the lighter end, largely by use of a 6in-thick bufferbeam in place of the 3½inch version at the other end. There were two fuel tanks mounted on the underframe, each of 170 gallons capacity. The locomotive bodies were straight-sided and box-like, built to the most restrictive loading gauge – not particularly elegant machines but, together with the dual-power arrangement, they really did have 'go anywhere' capability. They were the forerunner of today's 'bi-mode' trains, long before anyone had coined that phrase!

An initial batch of six, numbered E6001–E6006 and classified 'JA' under the coding system then in use, was built at Eastleigh between February and November 1962, partly for evaluation purposes. They were clearly considered successful, with thirty more being ordered in June 1963, and a further thirteen a little later in anticipation of requirements for the Bournemouth electrification scheme. Manufacture of these locomotives was awarded to English Electric, who turned them out from their Vulcan Foundry plant at Newton-le-Willows between 1965 and 1967. They were numbered E6007–E6049, and on completion, most worked from Cheshire down to the Southern under their own diesel power.

The 'production' models were classified 'JB', and there were some detail differences between them and the earlier JAs. Oval carriage buffers were initially fitted to the JAs, whereas the JBs had the round retractable type, later retrofitted to the earlier machines. Maximum speed differed slightly – 80mph on JA and 90 on JB. EE546 traction motors were used in place of the EE542 on the JAs – albeit still rated at 400hp – and changes were made to the bogie design, with the type being used subsequently on the REP and VEP units, together with later builds of Southern main-line multiple-units.

Features common to the whole fleet were drophead buckeye couplers and Pullman rubbing plates, together with high-level hoses in addition to the normal bufferbeam-mounted vacuum and air hoses, and multiple-unit control arrangements. Both air and vacuum brakes were fitted, together with the Electro-pneumatic (EP) system. This was all to meet a design requirement that the locomotives should be able to work in multiple with Southern Region EMU stock classes from 1951 onwards, in much the same way as the Class 33/1 diesels. Such was the flexibility of the braking systems that a locomotive could be marshalled between air- and vacuum-braked stock, and act as a 'translator' between the two systems. Train heating was electric, powered by the traction current supply when the locomotive was running on the live rail, and from the generator otherwise. The relatively limited capacity, however, meant that heating was only available in diesel mode when the locomotive was not on the move.

The locomotives worked across the Southern Region on a mixture of freight and passenger services, and they were regular performers on the Bournemouth line. They proved a useful stopgap in the early days of the electric service, working in multiple with TC units as cover for late deliveries of the REPs. Although it was intended that they would not venture far or move heavy loads while operating on diesel power, there was certainly the occasional instance of them working boat trains through to Weymouth in place of a Class 33. Under the TOPS classification system introduced in the early 1970s, the JAs became Class 73/0, and the JBs 73/1.

The final Class to consider is the 74, another electro-diesel, but in the best traditions of the Southern – and this scheme in particular – not a new build but an exercise in recycling! As mentioned previously, despite the obvious capabilities of the

Second-class accommodation in a 4-VEP unit. With two-plus-three seating, transverse luggage racks, and doors to each seating bay, there was little to distinguish this from contemporary suburban stock except, perhaps, for the orange window curtains and 90mph capability. *Crécy Archive*

73s, a need was identified for a more powerful locomotive, which could work trains on the electrified lines without delaying the REP/TC formations, but with the same ability to operate under diesel power when necessary. This was required particularly for the 'Ocean Liner' services and some freight trains, which would work over the non-electrified section from Northam Junction into Southampton Docks.

A Southern Region paper from 1965 shows that two options were considered to meet this requirement. The first was the development and construction of ten new electro-diesel locomotives, having a power output of 3,000hp on electric power and 600hp on diesel, at a total cost of £935,000. The alternative was to convert ten existing Class 71 electric locomotives, by installation of a diesel generator. Under the Kent Coast Electrification scheme a few years earlier, twenty-four of these locomotives had been built, with a power output of 2,552hp. With the reduction in freight and parcels traffic in Kent, some of these were now surplus to requirements, and would be available. The estimate for conversion was £425,000, although added to this was an additional sum of £459,000 to cover six new Class 73 locomotives to replace the converted 71s. This came to a total of £884,000, still less than the cost of new locomotives, and so it was decided to go ahead with conversion, the ten 'worst condition' Class 71s being selected.

The work was carried out at Crewe Locomotive Works, and was considerably more complex than simply installing a diesel generator within the existing locomotive body. As originally built, these locomotives had a 'booster' system, consisting of an internal electric motor driving a generator through a heavy flywheel. The idea was that the inertia in the flywheel would keep the generator turning and provide power to the traction motors while traversing breaks in the conductor rail, which could otherwise cause 'gapping' problems, especially when travelling at low speeds. This system was retained in the rebuilt locomotives, although the flywheel was replaced by a fan for traction motor cooling, the weight of the armatures and shafts being found sufficient to keep the generator turning. This meant, though, that space was at a premium within the

bodyshell. All of the additional equipment added weight as well, so major structural changes were made to limit the increase as far as possible. This involved a complete strip down almost to underframe level, and remodelling of the side panels to become load-bearing. This work was time-consuming and expensive, and with hindsight it might have been cheaper to build completely new locomotives! A different diesel generator was chosen from that in the Class 73s – a Paxman 6YJXL 'Ventura', of 650hp. This was a fast-running engine, which meant it was smaller and lighter than other types, an important consideration with these conversions. Other alterations were made to give these locomotives many of the same features as the 73s – retractable pick-up shoes, buckeye couplers and Pullman rubbing plates, and waist-level air and electrical jumpers – and like their smaller cousins they could work in multiple with all post 1951 EMU stock. As with the 73s, driving cab controls were duplicated to allow operation from either side, a feature that proved particularly useful on the Southampton dock lines. Prior to the introduction of the TOPS classification as Class 74, these locomotives were designated HB, the original 'donor' electrics having been HA.

The converted locomotives were initially numbered E6101 to E6110, and went into traffic between November 1967 and June 1968, all considerably later than the inauguration of the electrification scheme. The delays were due largely, as mentioned above, to the challenges arising from the conversion work, with the first example, E6101, taking thirteen months to complete. Once in service, the locomotives demonstrated that they were capable of carrying out the duties for which that had been built. They worked heavy passenger trains between London and Southampton docks at 90mph and more, as well as traversing the dock lines and shunting on auxiliary diesel power. They also worked some Channel Islands boat trains as far as Bournemouth, handing over there to a Class 33 for the onward run to Weymouth. Unfortunately though, they had an 'Achilles heel' in the form of a complex and fault-prone electronic control system. At the time, this was 'cutting edge' technology, and although it was later to be perfected on other locomotive classes, the 74s had the dubious privilege of being the prototype for an untried system, and reliability inevitably suffered. Other problems occurred with the cooling system, also controlled electronically, and a condition known as 'bounce', a pitching, end to end oscillation that was usually initiated by poor track, but resulted primarily from uneven weight distribution of the equipment within the locomotive. Once it started, it would frequently continue until the locomotive next came to a stand.

The gradual reduction in Ocean Liner traffic during the 1970s saw the 74s increasingly deployed on freight traffic, particularly coal trains from Chessington and Tolworth to Acton, which required a fair bit of mileage on diesel power. This put considerable strain on them, reducing reliability further still, and a decision was taken in 1976 to phase them out, meaning that no further general overhauls would be carried out, and locomotives needing repairs because of major faults or accident damage would be withdrawn. The last examples were taken out of service at the end of 1977, after only ten years of operation in their new guise.

It only remains in this chapter to mention the impressive versatility and interoperability the Southern enjoyed with its rolling stock on the Bournemouth line, powered and unpowered multiple-units working together, and diesel and electro-diesel locomotives doing likewise, and with multiple-units as well. In the REP and TC units, the auxiliary equipment (motor generators, EP brake compressors etc) was standardised, such that brake seconds, corridor firsts and buffet vehicles could be swapped between units, and a REP motor coach could be replaced by a TC driving trailer or a Class 73 locomotive (a feature that proved very useful at the time of electrification to Weymouth, described in a later chapter). The only limiting factors were that no more than two 1,600hp power units (motor coach or Class 73) could be included in a REP unit, while a TC brake second (which had the motor generator) could not provide power for more than four other vehicles.

Right: **The pioneer Class 73/0 (JA) electro-diesel, E6001, stands at Stewarts Lane in 1964. At this time, the locomotive still sported oval carriage buffers, later replaced by the round retractable version as fitted from new on the later Class 73/1 (JB).** *Christopher J Wilson Collection*

Opposite: **Interior view of a 4-VEP Driving Trailer Composite (DTCsoL) vehicle, looking towards the cab end. When at the front or rear of a train, the door seen open here was locked, with the vestibule beyond providing exclusive access to the driver's cab. When formed intermediately, both doors were unlocked and a through way provided for passengers to the next unit. The second-class seating in these units was generally in a two-plus-three layout, but at vehicle ends there were only two seats either side to provide sufficient access to the gangway, as seen here.** *Crécy Archive*

Class 73/1 (JB) electro-diesel locomotive E6048 leads the 09.21 Weymouth to Waterloo service into Southampton Central on 26 May 1967, around six weeks before the start of the full electric timetable. The train is one of the interesting ad hoc formations that could be seen at the time – the leading 4-TC unit has a REP trailer brake first and trailer buffet in place of its normal centre vehicles. *Christopher J Wilson Collection*

Electro-Diesels and TC units in full push-pull mode just south of Weybridge in early July 1967 – propelling a down service on the left, and hauling an up one on the right. *K P Lawrence*

On the interoperability front, no better example can be given than a peak service that worked at various times over the years between Salisbury, Eastleigh and Waterloo, the Salisbury portion comprising a Class 33/1 locomotive with a 4-TC unit, and the Eastleigh portion a pair of 4-VEPs, with attachment and detachment taking place at Basingstoke. Between Basingstoke and Waterloo, the whole formation – locomotive and EMUs – was controlled either from the cab of the Class 33 or from one of the VEPs, depending on which was leading. Allegedly, this train operated once with the locomotive coupled *between* the VEP and TC units, which must have caused some confusion for passengers waiting to board at any intermediate stations!

The pioneer Class 74 (HB) electro-diesel conversion, E6101 (formerly HA electric E5015), stands outside Crewe Works on 19 November 1967. *N E Preedy*

Class 74 in action – E6105 traverses the New Forest near Beaulieu Road with a Channel Islands boat train from Waterloo to Weymouth Quay, during 1968. The 74 will be replaced by a Class 33 diesel-electric at Bournemouth. *Christopher J Wilson Collection*

Class 33/1 diesel-electric locomotive D6520 passes Eastleigh with a 4-TC unit in tow during late 1966. Work has not yet started on the new buildings on the down island. *Christopher J Wilson Collection*

The redundant semaphore gantry at Worting Junction frames Class 33/1 diesel-electric locomotive D6520, as it hauls 4-TC unit 410 and an unidentified sister unit on a southbound working in early 1967. *Christopher J Wilson Collection*

In a view dominated by the clock tower of Southampton Civic Centre, Class 33/1 locomotive D6520 propels a Bournemouth to Waterloo service away from Southampton on 15 March 1967. The train is formed of 4-TC unit 413, with an unidentified 3-TC set leading. *John H Bird/ANISTR.COM*

In this undated view, a Class 33/1 locomotive propels a 4-TC unit from Weymouth into Bournemouth Station, where it will attach to a 4-REP unit for the run to London. *Kevin Robertson Collection*

4
1967

Test running over the newly electrified sections of the main line generally took place as soon as the power was switched on, between December 1966 and March 1967, and in the first two or three months there were regular test trips down the line from Wimbledon Park depot, using various combinations of suburban electric stock, sometimes accompanied by electro-diesel locomotives. As an example, a test train comprising locomotive E6052, 2-EPB units 5769 and 5672, and three coaches of 4-EPB unit 5129 made a trip from Wimbledon to Brockenhurst and back on 18 January, the same day that the Swaythling to Lymington Junction section was switched on.

Some local passenger services between Woking and Basingstoke were electrically worked from 2 January – using 2-EPB and 2-HAP units – replacing the diesel multiple-unit (DMU) shuttle services that had operated previously, and electric units first reached Bournemouth on 6 March, allowing some electric services to operate over the whole route from 3 April. Electric services started over the Lymington branch on 2 June, with 2-HAP units 6087 and 6102 in operation on the first day. Steam had already given way to DEMU operation three months earlier, to allow removal of the run-round facilities and other pointwork at Lymington Pier. However, deliveries of the new electric stock, especially the essential 4-REP tractor units, were delayed, with only units 3001–3 in service by the end of April, and so many of the early workings were ad hoc formations of Class 33 or 73 locomotives and TC units. Some of these had been temporarily re-formed with the buffet and brake-first vehicles from 4-REP units yet to be introduced, to ensure that a catering service could be provided. Things were not looking promising for the start of the new timetable in July.

Not quite 1967, but 19 December 1966. A test train from Wimbledon approaches Eastleigh, just a few days after this section was energised. The train comprises a pair of BR Standard 2-EPB units – 5739 leading – with three coaches of a SR design 4-EPB unit at the rear. *A D McIntyre*

One of the interim service alterations during the electrification work was the use of diesel multiple-units, loaned from the Western Region, on services between Basingstoke and Woking. One such example is seen here, pausing for custom at Winchfield with the 12.37 Basingstoke to Woking stopping service on 22 March 1967. The relaid and reballasted up fast line, with welded rails on concrete sleepers, can be clearly seen alongside. *John H Bird/ANISTR.COM*

However, new electric trains did not provide the only excitement on the Bournemouth line in the early part of the year. There was a huge variety of motive power in operation during the transitional period as steam was gradually run down. On the diesel front, the Southern's own Class 33s, together with Class 47s temporarily transferred from the Western Region, worked many services, including the Pullman 'Bournemouth Belle' on occasions. Western Region DMUs also put in appearances on shorter-distance services, notably between Woking and Basingstoke. Steam was still in widespread use, though, represented by 'West Country', 'Battle of Britain' and 'Merchant Navy' Bulleid Pacifics, along with various BR Standard Classes.

As spring moved into summer, the significance of this being the last steam-worked main line in the country was not lost on footplate crews, and it became clear that they were not going to let their charges go out without a show. Although a gradual rundown of maintenance had left many of these locomotives in poor condition – appearance wise apart from anything else – some fine runs were put up and many unofficial records broken as the final day drew near, taking full advantage of the newly relaid track and colour-light signalling. Numerous runs were claimed at speeds of over 90 and even 100mph, and many of these were authenticated by experienced recorders. As an example, on 26 June, 'Merchant Navy' 35003, *Royal Mail*, hauling a five-coach semi-fast service, achieved 106mph after passing Winchfield, and covered the 3.3 miles between there and Fleet in just 1 minute 56 seconds – an average of 102.4mph.

The last day of steam operation was Sunday, 9 July, but two 'Farewell to Steam' specials were run a week earlier, on 2 July, hauled by 'Merchant Navy' Class locomotives 35008, *Orient Line*, and 35028, *Clan Line*. Both had been specially cleaned for the occasion, and were turned out in immaculate condition, complete with their nameplates refitted. *Orient Line* left Waterloo at 09.55, and hauled an eleven-coach train to Weymouth, reaching a maximum speed of 90mph en route. On the return trip, the train was double-headed as far as Bournemouth with the addition of sister locomotive 35007, *Aberdeen Commonwealth*. *Clan Line* headed the second special on a round trip to Bournemouth, departing Waterloo at 12.20.

In the last months before the start of full electric working, Woking to Basingstoke shuttles were worked by electric stock, normally suburban units such as 2EPB 5662 seen here at Woking on 18 April 1967. The unit has arrived from Basingstoke and is leaving the station prior to crossing to the down slow line to form a return working, for which the headcode has been displayed somewhat prematurely. *Terry Phillips*

Friday 2 June 1967 was the first day of electric working on the Lymington branch, with 2-HAP units 6087 and 6102 doing the honours. Here, the pair await departure from Brockenhurst with the next shuttle, while their predecessor, Class 205 DEMU 1126, stands in the adjacent siding. *John H Bird/ANISTR.COM*

Five specials had originally been planned, but in the event just the two proved adequate, as demand was low due to poor publicity and high fares – £4 being charged for the return trip to Bournemouth behind *Clan Line*. Many passengers managed to enjoy steam haulage that day on other trains, but at normal fares, including the 09.33 excursion to Bournemouth and back, hauled by 'West Country' 34025, *Whimple*, and on the 19.36 Bournemouth to Waterloo service in the hands of 34037 *Clovelly*, which managed to reach London 25 minutes ahead of time!

In spite of the run-down of steam, well over 200 services were steam-hauled over the line during the following seven days. On Sunday, 9 July, a rumour was heard at Bournemouth that a number of Bulleid Pacifics were going to be retained as temporary cover while the new electric stock bedded in, but this quickly proved to be unfounded. That afternoon, 'Merchant Navy' 35030, *Elder Dempster Lines*, worked the very last steam-hauled passenger train on the Southern Region, the 14.07 Weymouth to Waterloo. This train was filled with enthusiasts from Bournemouth, many of whom had been hoping that this honour would have fallen to the last ever 'Bournemouth Belle' Pullman service, due to depart at 16.37, but in the event, this was diesel-hauled. The vast majority went for the 'bird-in-the-hand' approach, and got their last steam run on the up Weymouth train, which reached Waterloo 10 minutes early, at 17.46. From the following day, the remaining steam locomotives began to be moved to Salisbury and Weymouth for storage prior to being hauled to the breaker's yards for scrap.

The full electric timetable commenced on Monday, 10 July, having been postponed from a month earlier because of the late delivery of new rolling stock. There had been suggestions that it should be postponed further still, but this was quickly vetoed by those in charge. The remaining steam locomotives were in such a run-down state by this point, that there was a real danger of the service collapsing completely if any attempt was made to prolong their operation. In addition, the revised date applied not just to the Bournemouth service, but to the entire Southern Region timetable. This was a radical rewrite, intended to address – among other things – serious overcrowding on many commuter services, and it was based on detailed research and passenger surveys carried out over the previous three years.

Things did not get off to the best of starts, due to a combination of first-day 'teething troubles', and the ongoing rolling stock shortages. At least two of the 4-REP tractor units and one of the 4-TC trailer units were not available for service on the first day, and a number of the 4-TC units had been delivered in three-car formation, awaiting completion of the missing vehicles. This resulted in the continued operation of ad hoc formations, with Class 33 and 73 locomotives working with 4-TC units, some still including REP buffet cars and trailer brake-firsts. At least the Class 73s were available, unlike their troublesome larger cousins, the converted Class 74s. The first of these, E6102, did not leave Crewe Works until November 1967, meaning that the small number of Class 47 diesel-electric locomotives, which had been working on the route for some months, had to be retained to handle boat train traffic.

Full electric formation before the full electric timetable. On 24 June 1967, 4-REP unit 3007 – unusually marshalled at the 'country end' of the train – leads 4-TCs 417 and 414 into Southampton Central with the 15.35 service from Waterloo. *John H Bird/ANISTR.COM*

Above: **4-TC unit 403 brings up the rear of a Waterloo to Bournemouth train passing a rather sorry-looking Beaulieu Road station in the summer of 1967. The canopies have gone, and the single-storey buildings on each platform would later be demolished.** *Christopher J Wilson Collection*

Left: **Test trips with suburban and outer-suburban stock continued almost to the start of full electric working. This view on 2 July 1967 shows 2-HAP unit 6139 leading another of the same class past Steventon, the birthplace of Jane Austen.** *Christopher J Wilson Collection*

Teething troubles started with displacement of a live rail causing problems at Basingstoke. Potential for greater embarrassment arose from an inaugural civic luncheon held at Bournemouth, where attendees included Barbara Castle (Minister of Transport), Sir Stanley Raymond (Chairman of the British Railways Board) and David McKenna (General Manager of the Southern Region). This party travelled from Waterloo on the 10.30 Weymouth service, which arrived at Bournemouth around 10 minutes late, mainly because it was running close behind the 09.47 semi-fast service. This earlier train had left Waterloo at 10.00, and lost a further 4 minutes en route, largely due to a signal check near Basingstoke. However, it managed to recover some of the arrears impressively, with an actual running time to Bournemouth of 1 hour 58 minutes, against a schedule of 2 hours 7 minutes. There were further problems later in the day, with the 17.56 Bournemouth to Waterloo not leaving until 18.40, suffering serious signal checks between Farnborough and Woking and around Vauxhall, and finally arriving at Waterloo some 93 minutes late!

The Lymington branch also got off to a bad start, with the 2-HAP unit working the 05.30 Eastleigh to Lymington Town service failing at Brockenhurst. Bus substitution was instituted for the rest of the morning, with a train service not restored until midday.

Reliability of the 4-REPs was poor in the early days, with loss of pick-up shoes a fairly common problem. In part, this arose from the use of a particular safety feature for staff carrying out coupling or uncoupling of units – a large rubber mat that was placed over the live rail whenever the electrical and brake jumpers had to be handled on the 'non-platform' side. Unfortunately, the mats were not always removed when the operation was complete, with inevitable results! The other reason was that the initial design of shoe, which followed that used on the new Brighton line CIG and BIG units a couple of years earlier, proved not to be sufficiently robust for the sustained high-speed running on the Bournemouth line. A design feature of the shoes was that they should break off in the event of striking an obstruction, but early experience showed that it only required the slightest impact for this to occur, resulting in the loss of several at speed, a problem that was resolved by a redesign and use of different materials.

Some of the stopping services also suffered occasional disruption early on, when pre-war 2-BIL or 2-HAL units were inadvertently rostered on the Portsmouth to London stopping services that attached to a portion from Basingstoke at Woking. The latter were diagrammed for the new 4-VEP units or 2-HAPs, neither of which could couple to the earlier stock, meaning that the attachment could not take place!

The basic structure of the electric timetable has been mentioned earlier, but in detail the weekday off-peak service pattern from Waterloo was as follows:

xx.13 – Surbiton, Woking (portion detached for Portsmouth and Southsea), all stations to Basingstoke (62 minutes);

xx.30 (generally even hours only) – Southampton Central (70 minutes), Bournemouth (100 minutes), Poole, Wareham (connection for Swanage), Wool, Dorchester South, Weymouth (161 minutes). There was an additional 09.30 service to Bournemouth until 1 September, calling only at Southampton Central, and a 15.30 service for Southampton Central, Bournemouth, and all stations to Swanage, which ran all year.

xx.43 – Surbiton, Woking, Brookwood (portion detached for Alton), all stations except Southampton Airport to Bournemouth (174 minutes). This service was overtaken by the following xx.47 just beyond Woking and, on even hours, the xx.30 at Southampton Central.

xx.47 – Woking, Basingstoke (48 minutes), Winchester (67 minutes), Eastleigh, Southampton Airport (78 minutes), Southampton Central (86 minutes), Brockenhurst (connection for Lymington Pier), New Milton, Christchurch and Bournemouth (127 minutes). On even hours, these services continued to Weymouth, calling at almost all stations (most omitted Holton Heath off-peak) and taking 197 minutes from Waterloo.

The Lymington branch was served by a shuttle service from Brockenhurst, running at hourly intervals with some additional trains in the morning and evening. Similarly, Swanage had a shuttle service from Wareham, supplemented by the 15.30 from Waterloo and a train from Bournemouth at 18.25. Frequency was roughly hourly, but there were some two-hour gaps in the middle of the day.

On the main line, there were the usual evening peak variations to cater for commuters, as follows:

17.18 – Woking, Farnborough and all stations except Southampton Airport to Southampton Central (105 minutes);

17.30 – Basingstoke (45 minutes), Winchester (64 minutes), Southampton Central (78 minutes) and Bournemouth (108 minutes);

17.48 – Woking, Farnborough and all stations except Southampton Airport to Bournemouth (169 minutes);

18.11 – Winchester (63 minutes), Southampton Central (78 minutes) to divide. Front portion called at Brockenhurst (95 minutes) and Bournemouth (111 minutes). Rear portion called at all stations to Bournemouth and arrived 22 minutes later.

The last 'fast' service to Weymouth was at 20.30, arriving at 23.11, followed by the 20.47 semi-fast, arriving at 00.05. There were also mail and newspaper trains, leaving Waterloo at 22.52 and 02.45 respectively, but these had extended dwell times for loading and unloading at many stations en route, and the 22.52, for example, did not reach Weymouth until 03.32.

On weekdays, there were also three 'inter regional' trains, two from Birmingham New Street (one to Poole and one to Southampton Central), and one from York to Poole, starting back at Newcastle until 1 September.

The Saturday service largely followed the weekday off-peak pattern, but there were numerous extra trains through the summer to cater for the seaside holiday and day-trip market. Most of these ran until 2 September and were as follows:

07.55 Waterloo to Swanage;

08.00 Waterloo to Lymington Pier;

08.55 Waterloo to Weymouth;

09.25 Waterloo to Bournemouth;

09.55 Waterloo to Swanage;

10.00 Waterloo to Lymington Pier;

10.55 Waterloo to Weymouth (until 5 August);

11.25 Waterloo to Bournemouth;

11.55 Waterloo to Swanage;

12.05 Waterloo to Lymington Pier;

13.30 Waterloo to Bournemouth;

15.30 Waterloo to Bournemouth.

In addition to the through London services above and the shuttles from Wareham, Swanage had five direct services from Bournemouth, although one of these only ran until 2 September. There was also an additional late evening train to Bournemouth, leaving Waterloo at 23.47 and arriving at 01.46. Seven inter-regional trains ran to either Bournemouth or Poole, from starting

On 22 August 1967, 4-VEP unit 7716 leaves Woking with the Basingstoke portion of the 11.13 from Waterloo. The rear portion, for Portsmouth Harbour, was formed of a pair of 2-HAP units. Note the blue-painted window frames; later batches of these units were fitted with unpainted aluminium frames.
Terry Phillips

points as far afield as Bradford, Carmarthen, Liverpool, Sheffield, Leeds and Manchester. Most of these ran until 2 September, but the Bradford service finished on 12 August while the Manchester one ran until 16 September.

The Sunday pattern broadly followed that on other days, with services having the same departure times from Waterloo, and the same journey times. There were a few minor variations. The 08.30 Waterloo to Weymouth only ran until 3 September, and there was an additional 09.30 to Bournemouth until 15 October and from 7 April. The hourly service to Basingstoke at xx.13 did not run, meaning that stations from Woking to Basingstoke were served just once an hour, by the xx.43 slow Bournemouth train. The stations at Micheldever, Shawford, Millbrook, Redbridge, Lyndhurst Road, Beaulieu Road and Hinton Admiral had no Sunday service between 15 October and 7 April.

Swanage had ten trains on Sunday until 10 September and from 3 March, but during the off-season period in between these dates, it was served by a bus from Wareham, with just five round trips. Similarly, Lymington had an hourly shuttle from Brockenhurst until 17 September, and two-hourly thereafter. There were no inter-regional trains on Sundays.

In the up direction, the weekday off-peak pattern was a mirror image of the down, with departures and starting points as follows:

xx.13 from Bournemouth, all stations to Brookwood (portion attached from Alton), then Woking, Surbiton and Waterloo. Journey time 166 minutes, eight minutes less than the down working largely due to a shorter wait (for overtaking) at Southampton Central.

xx.27 from Basingstoke, all stations to Woking (portion attached from Portsmouth and Southsea), then Surbiton and Waterloo.

xx.35 from Weymouth (even hours only), Dorchester South, Wool, Wareham, Poole, Bournemouth, Southampton Central, London Waterloo. Journey time 165 minutes, 4 minutes longer than down, but the same timings from Bournemouth (100 minutes) and Southampton Central (70 minutes) to Waterloo. There was one additional service until 1 September, starting from Bournemouth at 11.40, and calling at Southampton Central and Waterloo in the same timings.

xx.42 from Weymouth (odd hours only), all stations except Holton Heath to Bournemouth, then Christchurch, New Milton, Brockenhurst, Southampton Central, Southampton Airport, Eastleigh, Winchester, Basingstoke, Woking, Waterloo. Journey time 202 minutes. On alternate hours, this train started from Bournemouth at xx.56.

The morning peak variations make an interesting comparison with today's timetable, and show how much working and commuting habits have changed during the intervening years. The earliest London arrivals possible on direct trains from

The shortage of 4-REP units in the early months of the electric service is reflected by this view at Woking on 22 August 1967. The 08.42 Weymouth to Waterloo service arrives at Woking formed of a pair of 4-TC units headed by electro-diesel locomotive E6019. It was only a few minutes late, despite the shortfall in power, but the advertised refreshment service from Bournemouth would not have been provided. *Terry Phillips*

various starting points were as follows:

Basingstoke – 06.59 (05.57 from Basingstoke);
Southampton Central, Eastleigh and Winchester – 07.59 (06.12 from Southampton Central);
Bournemouth and Brockenhurst – 08.20 (06.20 from Bournemouth);
Poole – 09.02 (06.35 from Poole).

It's unlikely that many would seriously consider commuting from Weymouth even today, but in 1967 you could not have reached Waterloo from there before 09.24, and that only by catching the 06.18 departure!

As with the evening peak services, there was some portion working going up in the morning. Two trains left Bournemouth at 06.30 and 06.52, the first calling at all stations to Southampton Central and the second running non-stop, where it attached to the first. The combined train departed at 07.24 and called only at Basingstoke en route to Waterloo, where it arrived at 08.40. The 07.35 from Weymouth combined with the 07.39 from Swanage at Bournemouth, departing there at 08.40 and running to Waterloo in the 'standard' time of 100 minutes, calling only at Southampton Central. The 07.57 from Bournemouth, which called at all stations to Brockenhurst and then Southampton Central, Southampton Airport, Eastleigh and Winchester, was notable for running non-stop from Winchester to Waterloo in just 58 minutes, departing there at 09.03 and arriving at 10.01.

The last through train of the day from Weymouth in 'standard' timings was the 19.35, arriving at Waterloo at 22.20, but as in the down direction there was the mail train, leaving at 22.35, and reaching London at 03.43.

On Saturdays, there were additional up services as follows, roughly balancing the down extras, and all running until 2 September:

08.47 Swanage to Waterloo;
09.10 Bournemouth to Waterloo;
10.05 Weymouth to Waterloo;
10.47 Swanage to Waterloo;
11.00 Lymington Pier to Waterloo;
12.10 Bournemouth to Waterloo;
12.47 Swanage to Waterloo;
13.00 Lymington Pier to Waterloo;
14.10 Bournemouth to Waterloo;
14.47 Swanage to Waterloo;
15.00 Lymington Pier to Waterloo.

Seven inter-regional trains ran as well, largely balancing workings of the southbound services. The Sunday service was broadly the same as that in the down direction.

A buffet and full restaurant service was provided on most of the fast and semi-fast services during the week, although

4-VEP units were not universal on stopping services in the early days of electric working. In this view at Southampton Central on 15 July 1967, a pair of 2-HAP units, led by 6165, set off for Waterloo with the 13.13 stopper from Bournemouth. *John H Bird/ANISTR.COM*

not west of Bournemouth, the catering vehicle being formed in the 4-REP units, which only operated between there and Waterloo. At weekends, the catering provision was restricted to 'light refreshments' rather than full meals, and was withdrawn from a number of trains from 2 September.

Overall, the timetable was classic Southern Electric – fixed interval, with a mixture of fast, semi-fast and stopping services. Frequency and ease of connections were two of its principal features. Every 2 hours, the xx.43 Waterloo Bournemouth slow service was overtaken by the xx.30 fast at Southampton Central, allowing passengers from stations between Waterloo and Southampton to connect into it for a quicker service west, while passengers from the fast could reach minor stations west of Southampton without travelling all the way from London on the slow service. The slow service on the alternate half hour, at xx.13, connected into the semi-fast service at Basingstoke, albeit with a 20-minute wait there. A similar connection between the slow and the two-hourly fast service was available at Southampton Central in the up direction as well.

Journey time improvements were the other important feature, and the timings by the two-hourly fast services represented reductions over the best steam-worked schedules of 10 minutes to Southampton, 20 to Bournemouth, 18 to Poole, and 19 to Weymouth. Interestingly, one of the most striking improvements was made by the Waterloo to Bournemouth stopping service. Although, at 2 hours 54 minutes, this was far from quick, it was a whole 61 minutes faster than the best steam equivalent, and all the more impressive given that those steam timings could be enjoyed just twice a day, while the electric service ran every hour.

Of particular note is that, from the start of the new timetable, every weekday, there were no fewer than 126 point-to-point timings between stations on the route averaging 60mph or more. Of these, the slowest were the 'standard' timings fast Weymouth services between Southampton and Bournemouth, covering the 28.26 miles in 28 minutes, at 60.56mph. The fastest slot was reserved for the up Bournemouth semi-fast services, which covered the 23.46 miles between Basingstoke and Woking in 19½ minutes, at 72.19mph.

Investment in the Bournemouth electrification had been justified on the grounds of reduced operating costs alone, before any account was taken of increased passenger numbers. Nevertheless, during the thirty-six weeks following the start of electric services on 10 July 1967, passenger receipts were 20 per cent up over the corresponding period in 1966.

There were many sad faces once the last steam locomotives had gone, and the electric services settled into a reliable routine. For regular travellers though, and commuters especially, this brought a much longed-for relief from the months of disruption, diversions and speed restrictions that the work had entailed.

5
The REP/TC Years

An unusual formation for a Waterloo to Weymouth service (according to the headcode) is seen in this view at Wimbledon during 1969. Class 33/1 diesel electric locomotive D6524 leads a 4-TC unit and the unique 8-VAB unit 8001, whose blue/grey buffet car – the seventh coach in the formation – is just distinguishable amongst the plain blue VEP vehicles. The circumstances are not recorded, but the combination would have had 4,550hp at its disposal! *Christopher J Wilson Collection*

As the 1960s drew to a close, the REPs and TCs had settled into a steady routine on the fast and semi-fast services, ably supported by VEPs on the slows. Helped by the superb alignment of the South Western main line, and the high installed power of the REPs, these trains showed what multiple-units could really do, and laid to rest once and for all the old myth that the Southern was running some sort of glorified tramway!

Sustained 90mph running was commonplace, and speeds of 100mph and more were regularly achieved on the fine racing stretches between Woking and Basingstoke, and onwards down through Winchester to Eastleigh. The 70-minute timing of the fast services to Southampton Central was easily within the stock's capability, and was frequently bettered, with start to pass times of 60 or 61 minutes between Waterloo and Northam Junction not uncommon. And while the section between London and Southampton was undoubtedly the best in alignment terms, these trains also made the most of the more curvaceous stretches further west, and there was frequently spirited running through the New Forest and west of Lymington Junction. It's probably no exaggeration to say that the performance of these fast services was not far behind that of the AC electrics and 'Deltics' on the West and East Coast main lines respectively.

The point-to-point timings of the semi-fasts were more challenging, but again, hard running could generally make up for any slack station work. The VEPs also proved themselves lively runners, and while not quite in the REP league, turned in some regular 90mph plus runs on some limited stop workings.

The much-delayed Class 74 electro-diesel locomotives began to appear in numbers early in 1968, with E6101 to E6104 all at various locations on the Southern Region by March. However, it was not until later in the year that further deliveries allowed the start of a gradual return of the loaned Class 47 diesels to the Western Region, with D1921 the first to go back. Availability of the 74s and the 4-REP units was still not as good as expected, though, resulting in the formation of the temporary 8-VAB unit, mentioned earlier.

The new timetable effective from 6 May 1968 to 4 May 1969 included few changes from the inaugural one of the previous year. The combined Bournemouth and Alton services now divided and attached at Woking rather than Brookwood, and a peak-hour working from Waterloo, the 18.11 to Bournemouth, was retimed to depart at 18.00. It made calls at Farnborough, Fleet, Winchester, Southampton, Brockenhurst and all stations to Bournemouth. It no longer detached a slow portion at Southampton, and running times were 69 minutes to Winchester, 83 minutes to Southampton, 100 minutes to Brockenhurst and 125 minutes to Bournemouth. A number of stations on the route were closed on Sundays between 14 October and 29 March; these were Micheldever, Shawford, Millbrook, Redbridge, Lyndhurst Road, Beaulieu Road and Hinton Admiral.

A minor accident occurred at Waterloo on 12 July 1968, involving the departing 11.47 Waterloo to Bournemouth service, formed of 4-REP unit 3006 propelling 3-TC 301. One vehicle of the TC unit became derailed; only minor damage resulted, and there were no injuries, but a temporary ban was applied to push-pull working from platforms 11 and 14.

There was some rationalisation of the track layout on the Swanage branch during 1968, with the line being singled throughout – apart from a passing loop at Corfe Castle – and the removal of run-round facilities at Swanage. In practice this caused no problems, as the shuttle service from Wareham was worked by a DEMU, while Swanage portions of through London services were formed of TC units and push-pull-equipped Class 33/1 locomotives. There was a minor hiccough on one occasion, though, when a standard Class 33/0 was inadvertently rostered for a Swanage service, which had to be hastily terminated at Wareham, with the passengers transferred to the next branch shuttle!

The interoperability of the Bournemouth line stock and the various locomotive classes mentioned earlier came into its own at times of disruption or diversion, a case in point being Sunday, 20 October 1968, when the main line was closed due to bridge works just north of Winchester. Bournemouth services were diverted via the Portsmouth direct line as far as Havant. Here, a Class 33/1 was attached, which powered the train over the non-electrified section from Portcreek Junction, where the Portsmouth line diverged, through Fareham and on to Eastleigh, where the live rail was regained. The train then continued to Bournemouth on electric power, while the locomotive returned to Havant with the next up service, working in push-pull mode as appropriate.

The all-blue livery applied to the REP and TC units from new did not wear well, the original eggshell finish deteriorating into a drab matt look, and repaints into the standard BR main-line livery of blue and grey began fairly early, with 4-TC units 401 and 404 and 4-REP 3001 all being done during 1968. A casualty

On the long, straight, quadruple track stretch between Basingstoke and Woking, 4-REP unit 3008, with a pair of 4-TCs in tow, races past Winchfield with a Weymouth to Waterloo service in the summer of 1970. *Christopher J Wilson Collection*

While carriage roofboards had become part of railway history, some Southern EMUs continued to carry small destination boards above the cab side windows into the 1970s. 4-REP unit 3008 sports one in this view, awaiting departure from Southampton Central with a Bournemouth to Waterloo service in August 1974. Also evident is how much smarter these units looked in BR blue/grey livery with full yellow ends. *Christopher J Wilson*

of this work was the cast aluminium double arrow logos fitted below the cab side windows. These were removed during repainting and replaced by a white transfer lower down in the blue area, although York Works continued to turn out new VEP units in blue, with the cast logos fitted.

Proposals were put forward in 1968 for further electrification of a number of diesel-worked routes throughout the Southern. These included Alton to Winchester, Branksome to Weymouth, Cosham to Fareham, and Fareham to both St Denys and Eastleigh. Instructions were given that none of the track on these lines should be relaid using type 'E' concrete sleepers, which could not accommodate the fixings for conductor rail insulators. In the event of course, the proposal for the first of these routes ultimately came to nothing, while the others had to wait at least twenty years for electric trains to arrive.

Coupling and uncoupling of REP and TC units at Bournemouth required clear communication between staff and traincrew at different points on the platforms. This was initially achieved by hand signals, but crowds of passengers at busy times made this increasingly difficult, and so staff were issued with compact 'walkie-talkie' radios, measuring around 8in by 4in, and carried for convenience on a neck or shoulder strap.

Although the REPs, TCs and VEPs largely monopolised Bournemouth line services, other EMU classes put in appearances from time to time, either as cover for shortages, or on special occasions. In September 1968, Brighton line 4-BIG unit 7036 – accompanied by a pair of VEP units – temporarily stood in for a REP/TC formation. BIG units were rare performers on the South Western Division at the time, as they had electric parking brakes, and South Western crews were not trained in the use of this feature. On 21 November, a ten-coach Basingstoke to Waterloo service was noted formed of 4-CEP unit 7187, and 2-HAP units 5629, 6024 and 6157, all nominally based in Kent. During May 1969, Central Division 4-CIG units 7324 and 7318, along with 4-BIG 7037 – all in ex-works condition – were used for Royal Train duties to take the Queen to engagements in Southampton and Portsmouth. In June, Central Division 4-VEPs 7734 and 7729 worked an excursion to Southampton Docks, diesel-hauled by Class 33 locomotive D6520 over the non-electrified section between Havant and St Denys. And in August, a Kent Coast 4-CEP unit, 7197, was noted on the main line in company with Class 73 locomotive E6010, undertaking trials to investigate the possibility of officially sanctioned 100mph running over the route.

Class 74 locomotive E6107 was in the wars on 7 September, when it caught fire at Hook while working an Ocean Liner Express to Southampton. It was rescued, after a delay, by Class 33 D6524, which was removed from a freight train at Basingstoke. It then hauled the boat train on to its destination, after a further pause at Basingstoke to remove E6107. Diesel haulage was reasonably common on boat trains around this time, primarily by Class 47 locomotives 'filling in time' between working Freightliner trains to and from the terminal at Millbrook.

The Swanage branch was to have been closed to passenger services from 6 October 1969, but this was postponed because of delays in granting licences to the operators of replacement bus services.

In late 1969, trials commenced between Totton and Bournemouth of a variation of the BR standard Automatic Warning System (AWS). Standard AWS had been in use for many years, and essentially provided drivers with a visual and audible warning in the cab when the train was approaching anything other than a green signal, ie, a double yellow, single yellow, or red. The driver had to acknowledge the warning within a set time, or the brakes were automatically applied.

Under the Total Operations Processing System (TOPS) adopted by BR in the early 1970s, the HB electro-diesel locomotives became Class 74. On 18 September 1974, 74 006 (formerly E6106) accelerates past Vauxhall with the 09.55 Waterloo to Weymouth Quay Channel Islands Boat Train. A locomotive change would take place at Bournemouth, with a Class 33 diesel-electric taking the train forward. *John Scrace*

Worting Junction, where the Southampton and Salisbury lines diverged west of Basingstoke, was subject to speed limits of 60mph (up) and 65mph (down). It was remodelled in early 1976 to allow trains to cross from the down fast to the down Southampton line, and from the up Southampton to the up fast, at the full 90mph line speed. This view shows work almost complete, although the original down direction 65mph crossover has yet to be fully removed. *Tony Woodforth/Kevin Robertson Collection*

Bournemouth line trains cross at Brockenhurst on 9 September 1976, two years before the resignalling and provision of the third line to Lymington Junction. Brockenhurst 'B' signal box and its semaphores are still very much extant, as 4-VEP 7716 arrives with the 11.12 Bournemouth to Waterloo stopper. An unidentified 4-TC unit leads the 09.46 Waterloo to Bournemouth semi-fast out of the down platform. *Noel A Machell*

The Southern had not installed AWS over much of its network (although it was fitted on the Bournemouth line as part of the 1967 electrification and resignalling), mainly because it had considered replacement of semaphore signals by colour-lights a higher priority. It was also concerned about the possible dangers of repetitive acknowledgement by drivers running continually under double yellow signals, a common situation on lines into or out of London in peak periods. AWS only classified signals as 'clear' or 'restrictive', the latter category making no distinction between caution or stop signals. It was possible that a driver in this situation, suddenly faced with a single yellow or red signal after a succession of double yellows, would automatically acknowledge the warning without actually taking any action to slow his train.

The experimental system was designed to address this concern, by use of a cab display repeating the individual aspects of signals being approached, and requiring the driver to acknowledge these by pressing the appropriate button. This, it was felt, would reduce the risk of repetitive acknowledgment arising from the generic warning used in standard AWS. A separate display showed the aspect of the last signal passed; this was also an improvement on AWS, which simply showed if it had been clear or restrictive.

The system was called SRAWS, these initials originally standing for Southern Region Automatic Warning System, later changed to Signal Repeating Automatic Warning System. The equipment was installed in 4-CIG unit 7437, with one of its driving trailer composite vehicles replaced with a 'spare' one from 4-VEP 7739, other vehicles of which had been used to form the temporary 8-VAB unit.

Although effective, SRAWS cost around three times as much to install as standard AWS, and development of the system was ended in 1975, when the BR Board decided that the standard AWS system should be installed throughout the Southern Region.

The weekend of 10/11 January 1970 saw track alterations at Northam Junction, with the curve on the main line being realigned, and the connection into Southampton Eastern Docks reduced to single track. Trains between Bournemouth and London were diverted between Southampton and Eastleigh via Romsey and Chandlers Ford, with Class 33/1 diesels hauling or propelling the REP/TC formations over this section. Some 'visiting' stock was again in operation, with 4-CEPs 7118 and 7126, and 4-BEPs 7006 and 7010 working services between Waterloo and Bournemouth in push-pull mode with Class 33/1 locomotives.

March saw completion of resignalling between Hampton Court Junction and Woking, filling the gap between earlier schemes in 1935 and 1937. Colour-light signals replaced the semaphores, and a new power signal box at Surbiton, commissioned over the weekend of 28 February to 1 March, replaced the existing box at the same location, together with those at Hampton Court Junction, Esher, Walton-on-Thames, Oatlands, Weybridge, Byfleet Junction and West Byfleet on the main line alone. The new Surbiton box also controlled sections of the Chertsey and Cobham lines, together with the whole of the Hampton Court branch.

On 1 June, Class 74 electro-diesel E 6109 – hauling a freight working from Temple Mills to Eastleigh – was involved in a collision with 2-EPB unit 5679 at Chertsey. There was damage to both the locomotive and the EMU, and three wagons were derailed. This resulted in the whole class being withdrawn from service for urgent checks on their brake block slack adjusters, but few problems were found and most of the locomotives were back in service just three days later, apart from E6109, which was sent to Crewe for repairs.

Dorchester South station had a curious layout, a hangover from the days of territorial competition between railway companies. The Southampton and Dorchester Railway – later absorbed by the London and South Western – had designs on continuing west towards Exeter, so temporarily built a terminus at Dorchester on an east–west axis. However, these plans were never realised, but a chord was built to join up with the Great Western's line to Weymouth, over which the LSWR was granted running powers. Subsequently, a platform was provided on the down side of the chord, but not the up. The original terminus remained, and in order to call at Dorchester up trains had to draw forward of the station and then set back into the platform. Remarkably, this arrangement continued until 1970, although ironically, push-pull working with Class 33/1 locomotives and TC units made the manoeuvre somewhat easier than with conventional hauled stock. A new up platform was built on the chord during the year, and some resignalling was carried out, centralising control of the area in Dorchester Junction signal box. Passengers continued to access the station via the original building and then use a wooden causeway to reach the platforms. It would be another sixteen years before this set-up was finally swept away, as part of the preparatory works for electrification through to Weymouth.

By early 1971, the 4-REP units were running on average twenty-five journeys per week over the 108 miles between Waterloo and Bournemouth, totalling some 2,700 miles. They visited Chart Leacon Works at Ashford for motor, bogie and brake overhauls every 60,000 miles, achieved in around twenty to twenty-five weeks. At 300,000 mile intervals, or roughly every two years, they went into Eastleigh Works for body repairs and a full repaint. Repainting of Bournemouth line units into blue/grey livery continued throughout 1971, with VEPs 7701–9 and 7716 of the original batch noted in these colours by the end of the year.

The fault-prone Class 74 electro-diesels had a relatively short service life – ten years at most following their conversion from Class 71. With a little over two months left in service, 74 005 passes Eastleigh with a Waterloo to Southampton Eastern Docks boat train on 1 October 1977. *Christopher J Wilson Collection*

The cranes of Southampton docks are framed by the magnificent signal gantry at the west end of Southampton Station in this view on 28 November 1977. The semaphores had around four more years to go at this date, the 4-TC unit leading the 11.46 Waterloo to Bournemouth rather longer. *Michael H C Baker*

July brought further visits by Ramsgate-based 4-CEP units, with a twelve-coach formation comprising units 7125, 7140 and 7187 working an excursion from Chiswick to Bournemouth on the 7th. More unusual was the appearance, on the 27th, of unit 7167 coupled to the hybrid 8-VAB unit 8001, on a Bournemouth service. The 4,000hp at this formation's disposal must have made for some lively running!

The Swanage branch was closed on 3 January 1972, although the section between Furzebrook and Worgret Junction, on the main line west of Wareham, was retained for use by trains carrying clay (and would later be used for oil from the Wytch Farm site).

The later batches of 4-CIG units, which were built primarily for Portsmouth and Reading services, put in appearances from time to time on the Bournemouth line, with units 7384, 7385, 7390, 7394, 7399, 7408 and 7414 in evidence on various services during January and February 1972. In March, 7381 operated services on the Lymington branch. An even more unusual substitution occurred on 14 April, during a work to rule, when the 09.42 stopping service to Bournemouth and 13.12 return were worked by suburban 4-EPB unit 5113, in place of the normal 4-VEP. It was perhaps fortunate that few passengers used this service over its entire length, as a shade under 3 hours in a train without toilets was not to be recommended!

The year 1972 saw colour-light signalling extended through the 'gap' between Bournemouth and Hinton Admiral, with the closure of the signal boxes at Christchurch and Pokesdown, and removal of the through roads at the latter. Control of this area was transferred to the box at Bournemouth.

The following year saw closure of the Alton to Winchester line, on 5 February, along with its intermediate stations at Medstead and Four Marks, Ropley, Alresford and Itchen Abbas. This line had, of course, featured heavily as a diversionary

57

route while the electrification works had been in progress, and there had been considerable opposition to its closure since this was first proposed some years earlier, led by Winchester Rural District Council and supported by the Alresford Chamber of Trade. The campaign included independent censuses of passenger numbers in an attempt to disprove those produced by BR, and resulted in the Minister of Transport ordering a second Transport User's Consultative Committee enquiry, the first time that this had happened in any closure proposal. Behind the scenes, an electric unit had been hauled over the route, to check pick-up shoe beam clearances, and BR promised that it would electrify the line if the closure proposal was ultimately rejected. Rumour even had it that material for the original Bournemouth Electrification had been so over-ordered that there was enough left to equip this route. In the event, though, all this was to no avail, and the closure went ahead as planned. Of course, the section between Alresford and Alton subsequently gained a new lease of life in preservation as the Mid Hants 'Watercress Line'.

An industrial dispute led to some further unusual formations on the Bournemouth line in early March. On the 7th, the 08.12 Bournemouth to Waterloo service was formed of Ramsgate-based 4-CEP 7202 in company with a pair of VEPs. On the 12th, the 12.56 Bournemouth to Waterloo and 15.47 return comprised a 4-VEP and a 4-CIG flanking a pair of 2-EPBs. The 8-VAB unit was also seen unusually working stopping services between London and Bournemouth.

A development during the summer was the permission, for the first time, of Class 33 locomotives on the Weymouth Quay line, which runs, tramway style, through the town's streets. Only 204hp shunting locomotives had been permitted previously, entailing a change of locomotive for the Channel Islands boat trains on arrival at Weymouth. The Class 33s carried a flashing warning light and a bell during their transit of the quay line, this equipment being fitted before they left the main line, and removed afterwards.

Like earlier schemes, the Bournemouth line enjoyed the 'sparks' effect, with commuters moving further out, and passenger numbers increasing generally. To cater for this increased demand, plans were made to increase the frequency of the fast Weymouth services to hourly from the start of the 1974 summer timetable. However, given the intensive diagramming of the REP/TC fleet, additional rolling stock was required. Orders were therefore placed with York Works in 1972 for a further four 4-REP units, three 4-TC units, and three additional refurbished TFK vehicles to make up the existing 3-TC units to four cars. Following on from the earlier sequences, the new REPs were numbered 3012–3015, the augmented 3-TCs renumbered from 301–304 to 429–431, and the new TCs 432–434.

The REPs followed the same pattern as the original batch, with new-build DMSO vehicles and rebuilt TBFKs and TRBs. One change, though, was the use of Restaurant Unclassified (RU) catering vehicles instead of the RBs of the earlier sets, and these required rather more extensive conversion work. As built,

The unusual arrangements at Dorchester South can be seen in this view on 3 August 1978. 4-TC unit leads the 12.38 Weymouth to Waterloo service out of the new up platform, provided in 1970, but the station building and original terminal platform is visible in the background. This remained in use, with passengers gaining access via a wooden causeway, until new up side facilities were provided in 1986. *John Scrace*

RUs had a kitchen, pantry, and a six-bay saloon seating thirty-three passengers, but no buffet counter at all. This therefore had to be created from scratch, in space freed up by losing two seating bays and the pantry. The result was a vehicle very similar to those in the original units, but there were some detail differences. There were no external doors between the seating area and the bar, and the counter itself lacked the angled end feature of the earlier conversions, continuing instead straight to a storage cupboard and bulkhead separating it from the seating area. On the corridor side, there were nine windows instead of seven in the RB conversions, one taking the place of the missing external door mentioned above, and the other where the RB vehicles had a second loading door on this side. One further, minor improvement over the original units was the fitting of double-glazed windows in all four vehicles.

The author recalls seeing an amusing item of graffiti in connection with the increased service frequency. There was obviously a publicity campaign to market the new timetable, much of this in poster form on stations. The one in question was actually observed somewhere on the London Underground, and contained the striking message, 'Every weekday, twenty-five Inter-City trains leave London for Southampton'. Underneath, some wag had written, 'only seven make it back!'

The Southern came in for some criticism for sticking to the now obsolescent Mark 1 coach design for these units. In particular, it was pointed out that the DMSO vehicles were the very last new Mark 1 vehicles to be built, at a time when the first Mark 3s were in service. This criticism was understandable to an extent, but needs to be balanced against the budgetary constraints that still applied, and the fact that commonality with existing stock clearly made sense. The introduction of this new stock finally allowed the withdrawal of the hybrid 8-VAB unit, with the VEP vehicles returning to their former incarnations and, as mentioned earlier, the catering vehicle scrapped.

Along with the new hourly frequency of the fast Weymouth services, all of the semi-fasts now terminated at Bournemouth. On alternate hours, when those services had previously run through to Weymouth, the fast service picked up its former stops and called at all stations beyond Bournemouth except for Upwey and Radipole (off-peak). This meant that Branksome, Parkstone, Hamworthy and Moreton saw their journey times to London cut by 28 minutes. Branksome was also served by all of the fast services, halving its service interval to hourly.

Few changes were made in the timetables effective from 5 May 1975, other than 4 minutes being cut from the Bournemouth to Waterloo semi-fast schedules. The Basingstoke and Bournemouth slow services were retimed to leave Waterloo a minute earlier, at xx.12 and xx.42. On Sundays, restaurant service was provided only on the 10.30 and 12.30 Waterloo to Weymouth services (and it would be withdrawn from all Sunday services from May the following year).

On 8 August, a railway police inspector travelling on a Bournemouth to London train considered that it was being driven erratically, and on arrival at Waterloo, went to the cab to speak to the driver. He found him unsteady on his feet, and urinating on to the track from the opposite side to the platform. The driver was taken to Kennington Police Station, where a sample indicated that his blood-alcohol level was over three times the legal limit for motorists. He appeared in court on 13 August, and was fined £25 for being drunk while conducting traffic on the railway (the maximum penalty at the time), and subsequently dismissed from his job.

Worting Junction, where the Southampton and Salisbury lines diverged west of Basingstoke, had always been considered a 'high-speed' junction, with 60mph (up) and 65mph (down) permitted through the crossovers in steam days, and through the earlier years of electric working. However, it represented the only restriction to sustained 90mph running from north of Woking to the outskirts of Southampton, and so remodelling was carried out in early 1976. New 'Y' formation crossovers were installed, allowing trains to cross from the down fast to the down Southampton line, and from the up Southampton to the up fast, at the full 90mph line speed.

No. 74 006 became the first of the troublesome Class 74 locomotives to be withdrawn, in June 1976, less than nine years after its conversion from a Class 71. Fire damage was the reason for its early demise, but its nine sisters had all followed it by the end of the following year.

From 2 May 1977, fast Weymouth services were 'thinned out' on Sundays, with departures from Waterloo at 08.30, 09.30 and 10.30, then 17.30, 18.30, 19.30 and 20.30. These trains all called additionally at Basingstoke and Winchester. On the hours when they did not run, the xx.46 semi-fast services ran through to Weymouth. These called additionally at Sway, Hinton Admiral and Pokesdown (replacing the stopping service which now ran only to Basingstoke), and took 195 minutes to reach their destination. On weekdays, three peak-hour semi-fast services from Waterloo – at 16.46, 17.46 and 18.46 – gained stops at Woking, having previously run non-stop to Basingstoke. On Sundays, the 22.46 Waterloo to Bournemouth was extended to Weymouth, taking the place of the 22.52 overnight mail train, which no longer ran on Sunday nights.

On 30 March 1978, the 09.12 Waterloo to Basingstoke service was involved in a curious accident at West Byfleet station. An empty stock train that had arrived at Woking earlier, ran back down the rising gradient, with no one on board, and collided with the Basingstoke train at around 15mph. Fortunately the signalman at Woking was aware of the situation, and had stopped the Basingstoke train by signal at West Byfleet, and warned the crew. Most of the passengers had been evacuated on to the platform before the collision took place, but the driver and three passengers sustained minor injuries. The investigating officer concluded that incorrect brake application by the driver of the empty train was the cause.

Signalling and track layout changes were made at Brockenhurst and Lymington Junction in October 1978. Hitherto, Lymington branch trains had worked over the up and down main lines between Brockenhurst and the junction. Under the new arrangements a third, reversible line was laid alongside the existing down line, allowing branch services – which normally used the down bay at Brockenhurst station – to operate completely independently of the main line, while

Lymington Junction itself ceased to exist and the signal box was abolished. At Brockenhurst, there were two signal boxes – 'A' at the east end, built in 1964, and 'B' at the west end. Colour-light signals were installed, 'B' box abolished, and control centralised in 'A' box, which was fitted with a new panel, and renamed simply, 'Brockenhurst'. Additional crossovers were laid in at both ends to allow reversible working over the up loop, and to maintain access to and from the Lymington branch from the main lines. Brockenhurst also took over control of the level crossing at Lymington Town, which was equipped with full lifting barriers and CCTV.

The 1979 timetable saw the first acceleration of the fast Weymouth services since electrification twelve years earlier. Departures from Waterloo were moved from the time-honoured 'half-past' slot to xx.35, and the trains ran to Southampton Central in 67 minutes (3 minutes faster), and Bournemouth in 96 minutes (4 minutes faster). Journey times in the up direction were 68 minutes and 97 minutes respectively. On weekdays, restaurant service was provided on virtually all fast and semi-fast services from the 06.46 to the 19.35 ex Waterloo, and the 06.20 to the 20.41 from Bournemouth. A buffet service was provided at weekends. Another major improvement was a later last train from Waterloo to Bournemouth on weekdays at 23.46, arriving at 01.55. Previously, the last weekday service had been the 21.46 (other than the 22.52 mail train), although there had always been a 23.46 on Saturday and a 22.46 on Sunday. There was, however, still a two-hour gap on weekdays before this new last train, and it would be some years before that was plugged.

The operational flexibility of the REP and TC units came into its own on 2 and 8 August when a special formation was made up to convey members of the Royal Family to Portsmouth and Southampton docks. The buffet and brake first vehicles from 4-REP unit 3008 were topped and tailed by the DTS vehicles from 4-TC 416, the whole ensemble being powered by locomotive 73 142.

On Saturdays through the summer of 1980, Channel Islands boat trains were frequently double-headed by pairs of Class 73 locomotives between Waterloo and Bournemouth, a single Class 33 diesel working the train between there and Weymouth. These workings would have been handled by the more powerful Class 74s before their demise.

While the REPs were now generally very reliable in service, the traction motors were susceptible to ingress of and damage by powdery snow. One motor coach of unit 3004 was experimentally fitted with semi-enclosed motors in an attempt to solve this problem for a period during 1980–81, but this adaptation was not extended to any other units. Instead, a simpler solution was achieved by marshalling the REPs in the centre of the formation, sandwiched by the TCs, which gave a degree of protection when such conditions were forecast.

On 29 July 1981, the Prince and Princess of Wales travelled down the line to their honeymoon destination at Broadlands, near Romsey. The special train was formed of a Mark 2 first open, a Mark 1 brake corridor composite, and the Southern Region General Manager's saloon, in which the couple travelled. Motive power was provided – appropriately – by Class 73 locomotive 73 142, *Broadlands*.

Further resignalling work during 1981 replaced the remaining mechanical signalling between St Denys and Totton – including the magnificent semaphore gantry at the west end of Southampton Central station – together with the lines to Romsey and Fareham. Control was transferred to new panels in Eastleigh signal box, which was extended to accommodate them. This resulted in the closure of mechanical signal boxes at St Denys, Mount Pleasant Crossing, Northam Junction, Southampton Central, Millbrook, Redbridge and Totton on the main line, together with the crossing boxes at Adelaide Road, Chapel Crossing and Canute Road on the line into the docks, Romsey on the Salisbury line, and Woolston, Netley, Swanwick, Botley and Fareham on the two routes to Portsmouth. The curve in the main line at Northam was realigned to allow the 15mph speed restriction to be raised to 25mph, and reversible working was introduced over some lines between Northam and Millbrook.

A negative point during the same year was the withdrawal of full restaurant services from 5 October; these had been a feature of the route since electrification and before. A buffet service continued to be provided on most services, however, and with no changes to the kitchen equipment in the catering vehicles it was still possible to enjoy such delights as freshly toasted bacon sandwiches!

Many services were halted by a two-day ASLEF strike on 13 and 14 January 1982. The first train out of Weymouth the following day ran into a 10ft icicle that had formed in Bincombe Tunnel, causing damage to the windscreen and minor injuries to the driver's hands. After coming to a stop due to the release of the driver's safety device, the train continued to Dorchester, where minor running repairs were carried out, and then on to Bournemouth.

During the evening of 9 December 1982, a Waterloo to Bournemouth service ran into a pair of trees that had been brought down by high winds across the line near Fleet, The two leading vehicles, the DTSO and TBSK of 4-TC unit 428, were completely derailed but, remarkably, all vehicles remained upright. The driver sustained injuries, but there were none to passengers. The derailed vehicles required replacement of their bogies, and were not returned to service until 13 January the following year.

Between 1983 and 1985, major engineering work was carried out in Southampton Tunnel, necessitating single-line working for long periods. The work, which cost £4.5 million, included the laying of a 1 metre-thick concrete floor from end to end, and partial relining of the walls. In the timetable effective from 16 May 1983, 2 minutes were added to the running times of the down fast and up semi-fast services. From the same date, the last two fast Weymouth services in each direction – 20.35 and 21.35 ex Waterloo, and 18.34 and 19.34 from Weymouth – were withdrawn.

The station at Radipole, between Upwey and Weymouth, was unofficially closed from 31 December 1983. Although the Department of Transport had not formally given consent at this point, the wooden platforms were considered unsafe, and

Stopping services meet at Hinton Admiral, 16 June 1979. On the left, an unidentified 4-VEP unit calls with the 11.42 Waterloo to Bournemouth, while sister unit 7845 approaches with the 14.12 Bournemouth to Waterloo. These services had long ceased to be monopolised by the 'pioneer' VEPS 7701–20, 7845 being one of the third batch delivered during 1972. *D Kimber*

the expenditure required to make them so could not be justified. Consent was given in January, and the station was formally closed on 6 February.

On 17 April 1984, the Woking to Basingstoke section played host to some unusual stock in the form of the new Gatwick Express Mark 2 stock units 8302, 8205 and 8314, topped and tailed by Class 73 locomotive 73 132, and Gatwick Luggage Van 9105. The train spent the day carrying out high-speed test runs, despite it being only a month before the new Gatwick service was due to start.

The Waller's Ash loops between Micheldever and Winchester were around 1½ miles long, running between the sites of the former Weston and Waller's Ash East signal boxes. A bridge towards the southern end of the loops was assessed as being in poor condition under the main lines, while the sections under the loops were still sound. The problem was dealt with by shortening the loops at their southern ends, and slewing the main lines gently outwards to use the former loop bridge decks, before returning to their original formation. The work was carried out during late 1984 and early 1985, and required some single-line working while it was in progress. One downside of this change was a reduction in the capacity of the loops, which had previously had signals midway along their length, and could accommodate two freight trains one behind the other.

In the early hours of Saturday, 26 January 1985, a collision occurred near Micheldever. It involved the 03.30 Bournemouth to Woking staff train, formed of 4-VEP units 7754 and 7703, and 4-CIG unit 7395. The train ran into a chalk fall in the steep-sided cutting between the two Popham tunnels as it was accelerating away from the stop at Micheldever. Although it was not derailed, it suffered damage to a number of its pick-up shoes, losing power and coming to a stand just on the London side of the northern tunnel. Having established the cause of the problem, the train crew reported the position to Basingstoke signal box and requested assistance. The driver then used a short-circuiting bar to ensure that the traction current was off, before removing the damaged shoe from the leading bogie. Some of the railwaymen who were travelling as passengers got off and assisted the train crew, primarily by securing the other damaged shoes so that the train was safe to move.

Royal Train to Southampton Docks awaits departure from Waterloo on 8 August 1979. The train is formed of the buffet and brake-first vehicles from 4-REP unit 3008, topped and tailed by the DTS vehicles from 4-TC 416. Immaculately turned out Class 73 electro-diesel 73 142 provided the motive power. *John Scrace*

Class 33 locomotive 33 104, which had been running light from Salisbury to Basingstoke, was sent to assist, running 'wrong line' from Worting Junction towards the failed train. The locomotive was driven at around 50mph as far as Litchfield Tunnel, about a mile from the failed train, where speed was reduced to between 25 and 30mph. The driver was expecting to encounter detonators and someone displaying a red hand lamp some 300 yards from the front of the train, and was confident that he could stop safely from 30mph or so within this distance. Unfortunately, neither the detonators nor the warning light were present, and to exacerbate matters, the headcode panel on the front of unit 7754 was not illuminated either. By the time the failed train came into view, there was no time even for a full emergency brake application to have any effect, and the collision occurred with the locomotive still travelling at around 30mph.

The cab of the locomotive was badly crushed in the collision, and both the driver and his assistant were trapped in the wreckage and sustained injuries, these being relatively serious in the driver's case. Damage to the failed train was minor by comparison, although some passengers suffered minor injuries and shock. There were no fatalities. All the injured persons were removed from the site by ten o'clock in the morning, and clearance of the line was complete and normal working resumed by three in the afternoon.

In his report, the inspecting officer identified three main causes for the accident:

The failure of the driver of the failed train to put down detonators and display a red hand lamp 300 yards ahead of his train, to warn the driver of the assisting locomotive. While observing that the actions of railwaymen travelling as passengers in assisting the train crew were entirely understandable, he felt that they may also have contributed to some confusion in deciding who was responsible for doing what;

Excessive speed on the part of the locomotive driver, who should really have slowed to a walking pace once he had passed Litchfield Tunnel, as well as sounding his horn at regular intervals;

Most seriously, the failure of the Basingstoke signalman to obtain an assurance from the train crew that the detonators and red lamp were in place *before* he allowed the assisting locomotive to set off 'wrong line'.

An unfortunate contributory factor was the apparent failure of the headcode lights on the passenger train. When traction current is lost, these lights, together with others on the train – including those illuminating the driver's instruments – are powered by a back-up battery, which in turn is kept charged by the motor generator set. However, on unit 7754, the fuse in the charging circuit had 'blown' some time previously, and the battery had become discharged, with this fault going undetected.

The main recommendations in the report were that amendments should be made to sections of the rule book, although the inspecting officer also suggested that a consistent approach should be taken to the fitting of headlamps to locomotives (some classes had them, but not the 33s). In respect of the specific accident site, robust wire fences were subsequently installed along the 'cess' between the two Popham tunnels, to contain any future chalk falls and prevent them from obstructing the line.

Work began on the £500,000 rebuilding of Weymouth station during the summer of 1985, and was completed the following year. The original six-platform station with its extensive facilities had been in a run-down state, and was no longer fit for present-day requirements. Its replacement was centred on the lengthy 'excursion' platforms 5 and 6, now renumbered 2 and 3, with an additional shorter platform 1 – normally for use by Bristol services – alongside. Everything to the west was removed, and the site levelled to provide space for retail development and parking. A new 'L'-shaped single-storey building was provided, housing a ticket office, toilets and other facilities. The signal box remained operational for the time being, but was taken out of use two years later, with control being transferred to the panel in Dorchester South box.

The REP and TC units were reclassified under the TOPS system from May 1986, their former classifications of 430 (REP) and 491 (TC) changing to 432 and 438 respectively. This also resulted in the units being renumbered in new series, the REPs from 3001–3015 to 2001–2015, and the TCs from 401–434 to 8001–8034.

Although the Southampton Tunnel work had been completed in 1985, the 2 minutes added to the up semi-fast and down fast services in 1983 were not taken off, but added to the opposite direction counterparts as well in the May 1986 timetable. This was to accommodate additional station calls, at Clapham Junction on the semi-fast services, and at Southampton Airport on the fasts, ending nineteen years of regular scheduled non-stop running between Waterloo and Southampton. The fasts, however, did not start calling at the airport until 29 September, following completion of a new station building containing a ticket office and other facilities. Extensive car parking was also provided for 330 vehicles, the station now being close to junction five of the M27 motorway, the section between junctions four to seven having opened in 1983. To coincide with this major upgrade, the station name

One of the summer Saturday 'extras', the 12.05 Lymington Pier to Waterloo, passes Worting Junction on 9 August 1980, with 4-CIG unit 7340 leading. The 90mph crossovers laid in here four years earlier can be clearly seen. *D Kimber*

was changed to the slightly cumbersome title of 'Southampton Parkway for Southampton (Eastleigh) Airport', although only the first two words appeared in timetables.

The 18.10 Waterloo to Yeovil Junction and Bournemouth service was one of the mixed diesel/electric workings, normally formed Class 33/4-TC/8-VEP, with the VEP units detaching at Basingstoke. However, on 7 November 1986, the Bournemouth portion was formed of 4-TC unit 8018, and 4-REP 2017. The Class 33 and the 4-REP between them produced a total of 4,750hp, and not surprisingly, this super-powered combination put up a spirited performance!

In 1987 there were major improvement works at three of the route's most important stations – Basingstoke, Winchester and Southampton. At Basingstoke, this included a new car park, a new thirty-two-screen passenger information system, modern toilets, and general repainting and renovation. Completion was marked by a 'Rail Week' from 19 to 27 September, with exhibitions of modern locomotives and rolling stock, vintage road vehicles, and model railway layouts. Other events included guided tours of the 1967 power signal box, and return trips to Woking on the preserved 2-BIL and 4-SUB units.

At Winchester, the car park was improved, the roof on the down platform was renewed, and repainting was carried out. Improvements were also made to the ticket office and travel centre, with a new glazed entrance incorporating automatic sliding doors, terrazzo tiled flooring, and induction loops at the ticket windows. Staff accommodation was upgraded, and the station frontage saw the canopy re-erected and the clock restored and returned to its original position on the roof, this latter work being funded by a grant of £35,000 from the Railway Heritage Trust. The Mayor of Winchester unveiled a plaque on 22 July to mark the completion of this phase of the work, further improvements to the station forecourt being planned for the future.

The work at Southampton involved enlargement of the ticket office on the Blechynden Terrace (north) side, improved toilets on both sides, and the provision of a travel centre and improved staff accommodation. Landscaping work was carried out in the forecourt, along with the planting of shrubs and trees. The station was repainted, as was the public footbridge at the London end, this being embellished with representations of nautical signal flags spelling out, 'Welcome to Southampton'. The work on all three stations came to a total cost of more than £2 million, with funding coming from BR, Hampshire County and local district councils, and commercial partners.

Extensive work was carried out during the 1980s to remove blue asbestos, originally fitted as insulating material, from the Southern's fleet of 1960s EMUs. It was initially thought that the 4-VEPs had been built without it, but this proved not to be the case for the 'pioneer' Bournemouth line units, 7701–20. These units therefore began visiting British Rail Maintenance Ltd (BRML) at Eastleigh from 1987 to have the material removed. At around the same time, the class underwent a similar renumbering exercise to that carried out earlier on the REPs and TCs, the number series changing from 77xx to 30xx.

Eastleigh also undertook a major facelifting programme on the VEP fleet generally starting in 1988, the most significant aspect of this work being conversion of part of the large van space in the MBSO to form an additional passenger saloon seating eighteen passengers. New seat moquette, fluorescent lighting, and a public address system were also fitted throughout. Another consequence of this work was yet a further renumbering exercise, with completed units now in a 34xx sequence. Unit 3168 was the first to be so treated, entering Eastleigh early in 1988 and emerging, completed and renumbered as 3421, in March of that year. It was put on display at Waterloo on 24 March, and also made an appearance at the Bournemouth depot open day a few days later.

The mid-1980s saw the reorganisation of British Rail into business sectors, with the Southern Region joining parts of the Eastern, London Midland and Western Regions to become the new London and South East (LSE) sector. Apart from a new brown and orange livery – dubbed 'Jaffa Cake' – applied to some Southern CIG and CEP units, along with the Eastern's Class 309s, there was little outward evidence of the change, certainly on the Bournemouth line.

More obvious change came in June 1986, however, with the transformation of the LSE sector into 'Network SouthEast', under the inspirational leadership of its director, Chris Green (who had held various British Rail management roles, including manager of ScotRail immediately prior to this post). This time the outward evidence was hard to miss – a striking new livery of red, white, blue and grey stripes with an 'upsweep' at unit ends, together with a major rebranding programme for stations, exemplified by bright red lamp posts and platform seats. Numerous branding and marketing initiatives were pursued, including individual names for lines of route, and the 'Network Card' that for an annual fee allowed holders and three adult travelling companions a 33 per cent discount on off-peak fares, and a flat fare of £1 each for up to four children.

The Southern's principal main lines – to Ramsgate, Dover, Brighton, Portsmouth, Bournemouth and Exeter – had gradually dropped off the 'Inter-City' map during the sectorisation programme. Instead, Network SouthEast introduced the 'Network Express' designation, denoted by the headnote 'NE' in timetables, to indicate the fastest trains running on these routes, and both the fast and semi-fast services on the Bournemouth line fell into this category. Unfortunately, unlike the Inter-City product, which became rapidly more consistent, Network Express did not guarantee any particular type of stock – be it high- or low-density seating – or even a catering service, and so it began to lack any real meaning as a category. And as we shall see, imminent developments on the Bournemouth line would make these inconsistencies even more stark. These same developments also ensured that relatively few of the REP or TC vehicles would make it into the new livery, although they all carried the red, white and blue NSE 'flash' on the coach bodysides and the unit end gangway doors, together with 'Solent and Wessex' route branding.

6
On to Weymouth

As early as 1984, consideration was being given to future options for the Bournemouth line. The use of largely refurbished stock, while an economical choice in the 1960s, meant that not only did it now compare very unfavourably with that in use elsewhere on the British Rail network, but much of it was approaching life expiry – it's worth recalling that twenty-nine of the refurbished vehicles used in the 4-TC units had originally been built in 1951! The costs and benefits of various solutions were considered, including the continuation of the existing push-pull arrangements but with new stock, or splitting the service into London to Bournemouth and Bournemouth to Weymouth sections, with the latter worked by diesel multiple-units. The case in favour of electrification to Weymouth was fairly marginal, but it had the advantage of avoiding expenditure on new diesel locomotives or multiple-units, which tipped the balance in its favour. The decision was therefore taken to extend the live rail over the 32-mile stretch from Branksome to Weymouth, and to provide new electric stock, although even here there were two proposals on the table, described further below.

Approval for the scheme was given in January 1986, with electric services planned to start in May 1988. The budget was £53 million, of which £37 million was for the new rolling stock. The official start of work was marked by a ceremony at Poole on 6 October 1986, in which the Secretary of State

Track laying in progress on Upwey Bank, between Weymouth and Dorchester, on 22 March 1987. Conductor rail is also in place on the down line, just visible below the ballast wagons.
Roland Groom

for Transport, John Moore, MP, and the Mayor of Poole installed a gold-painted insulator. This was followed by the Mayors of Bournemouth and Weymouth laying a length of conductor rail. Mr Moore, together with BRB Chairman Sir Robert Reid and SR General Manager Gordon Pettitt, had travelled from London on board inspection saloon 975025, hauled by locomotive 33 110, which was fitted with a commemorative headboard. After the conductor rail ceremony, interior mock-ups of the new rolling stock were unveiled, these having been installed in a former RB catering vehicle.

Engineering and associated works were not as extensive as they had been on the original Bournemouth scheme, although to reduce maintenance costs, the line was singled for around 5 miles between Moreton and Dorchester South. This section was controlled from a panel in Dorchester South signal box, commissioned during 1985, which also took over control of the junction with the former Western Region line from Castle Cary. The existing signal boxes remained in use at Weymouth (until its closure in 1987), Wool, Wareham, Hamworthy, Poole and Branksome, and signalling alterations were made at both Poole and Wareham to allow trains to turn back towards Bournemouth.

Power was taken from the grid at Wareham and Redlands, between Upwey and Weymouth, and fed to six substations at Poole, Hamworthy, Worgret Junction, Winfrith, Dorchester and Redlands. The substation at Branksome was extended, and the whole area supervised from the existing control room at Eastleigh. Budgetary constraints meant that power was taken from the grid at 11kV, rather than the 33kV of earlier schemes. This imposed limits on the capacity of the supply, which meant that electric trains over the section from Branksome to Weymouth were normally limited to a single five-car unit of the new Weymouth stock, or two conventional four-car units, and a maximum of five such trains at a time were permitted west of Wareham.

A new station building was provided on the up side at Dorchester South, replacing the old one on the original alignment, and the down platform was extended. A new footbridge was also erected, allowing the existing subway to be closed. There were some complaints locally about the reduced access this provided to the down platform for disabled passengers, but new reversible working arrangements meant that all but three down trains daily were now scheduled to call at the up platform, and it was considered that 'suitable advice' could be given to any passengers affected. The new facilities were officially opened on 25 November 1986. Elsewhere, platforms were extended at Poole, Wool, Moreton and Upwey.

Other work carried out to ready the route for the new trains involved raising speed limits further up the line, creating the first officially sanctioned 100mph sections on the Southern electric network. Initially, these covered from a point just west of Farnborough to a couple of miles east of Basingstoke, Worting Junction to Eastleigh (down line only), and Brookwood to Byfleet and New Haw (up line only, and excluding Woking station), but further stretches would be approved later.

Improvements were also made to Bournemouth depot, where the new stock would be serviced. An extension was built, 156 metres long by 18.4 metres wide. Numbers one and three roads were provided with inspection pits for their full length of 236 metres, each capable of accommodating a ten-coach train of the new stock. Number two road was removed and the central floor lowered, while number four remained as the 'lifting' road. Externally, new carriage washing facilities were installed, capable of operation at temperatures down to -4°C, and a 'flush-down' apron was provided for cleaning and unblocking of train toilets.

Current was switched on over the Branksome to Weymouth section on 11 January 1988, with a special ceremony to mark the event being held at Wareham station on that day. Gordon Pettitt, SR General Manager, was present, and asked one of thirty local schoolchildren who attended to pull a symbolic lever, which triggered a row of 'representative' flashes between the platforms. One purpose of the event was to publicise the potential dangers of trespassing on the newly electrified line, but a lighter note was also struck by reference to the provision of twenty-eight special safe crossings for badgers in the area.

Modernisation at Weymouth. The new station building is complete, and conductor rails are in place in this view on 30 January 1988. Class 33/1 diesel-electric locomotive 33 101 stands at the buffer stops in company with a 4-TC unit. *John H Bird/ANISTR.COM*

The first electric train over the newly electrified section was a test working on 1 February 1988, formed of 4-CEP units 1611 and 1621, accompanied by Class 33 locomotive 33 106. It is seen here after arrival at Weymouth. *Roland Groom*

Platform extension work and modifications to the signal box in progress at Wool on 17 February 1988. A pair of 4-TC units, led by 8104 and propelled by Class 33/1 diesel-electric locomotive 33 110, arrives with a Weymouth to Waterloo service. *John H Bird/ANISTR.COM*

The new station building at Dorchester South, photographed on 17 February 1988. A London-bound service is departing, unusually with Class 33/1 locomotive 33 108 sandwiched between two 4-TC units, 8026 at the rear. *John H Bird/ANISTR.COM*

The first train to venture over the electrified section to Weymouth was a test working on 1 February, formed of a pair of Ramsgate-based 4-CEP units, 1611 and 1621, accompanied by locomotive 33 106 as a back-up in case of problems. The first revenue-earning electric train to Weymouth was a bit of an impromptu event, formed of a 4-VEP unit on 28 February. Engineering work was in progress between Eastleigh and Basingstoke, requiring diesel working of electric services over the Eastleigh/Romsey/Salisbury diversionary route. This resulted in a shortage of Class 33/1 diesels to work TC units between Bournemouth and Weymouth, so the 4-VEP came to the rescue!

Turning to the rolling stock, the initial option considered was for five-car units each comprising four new vehicles – three open standards and a driving trailer composite – coupled to a REP DMSO vehicle. This would be rebuilt internally to house the guard's office and luggage area, together with a small buffet. It was recognised that these REP vehicles would reach life expiry by around 2000, at which point new driving motor vehicles would be built to replace them. However, this plan was ultimately rejected in favour of completely new stock – twenty-four five-car EMUs utilising the main-line Mark 3 bodyshell. This represented a step change in design for Southern multiple-units, bringing modern facilities such as air-conditioning for the first time. British Rail Engineering Ltd (BREL) had previously turned out a batch of generator vans for use in locomotive-hauled trains operated by Iarnrodd Eirean (Irish Railways), and this design had the required structural strength to be used as a motor coach, carrying all the necessary equipment beneath the vehicle floor. Another innovation originally developed for Irish Mark 3 vehicles were power-operated doors, meaning that Bournemouth line travellers would be excused the practice of lowering the droplight to open the heavy wraparound swing doors of earlier Mark 3s.

The new units were designated Class 442, and later acquired an 'unofficial' Southern coding of 5-WES, for 'Wessex Electrics'. The formation was Driving Trailer Standard (DTS – 'standard' having supplanted 'second' as a class designation in 1987), Trailer Standard Wheelchair (TSW), Motor Buffet Luggage Standard (MBLS), Trailer Standard (TS) and Driving Trailer Composite (DTC). In appearance, the vehicles were very similar to standard Mark 3 coaches, except for the Driving Trailers, whose outer ends had a vaguely streamlined shape with wraparound windscreens and a centre gangway with buckeye coupling beneath. Standard Southern waist-level multiple control and brake jumpers were provided below the windscreens, though concealed behind contoured covers. There was also a standard power jumper and brake hoses at bufferbeam level, to allow locomotive haulage over non-electrified diversionary routes. Dot matrix route indicators were fitted above the gangway doors, but these were very small and difficult to read from any distance, and they fell into disuse after the units had been in service for a while, and were eventually removed during 1991–92.

Internally, all standard-class vehicles were fitted with a new design of two-plus-two seating, some in bays around tables, but with a high proportion in 'airline' layout. While toilets were generally in the same locations as on other Mark 3s, the luggage stacks opposite them were sacrificed to provide additional seating bays. Some internal decoration was provided in the form of works commissioned from artist Edward Pond, depicting various scenes close to the route, such as Bournemouth Pier, Chesil Beach, Lulworth Cove and Durdle Door. In standard class, these took the form of murals on the saloon end walls, while in first they were decorative panels on the compartment partitions. There was also an amusing hint of 'class distinction' in that the artist's first name was signed as 'Edward' in first class, and 'Eddie' in standard!

Looking in more detail, the DTS had the driver's cab, an entrance vestibule (normally out of use for passengers behind the 'active' cab), a saloon seating seventy-eight passengers, and a second vestibule with access to the toilet. This vehicle weighed 39.06 tonnes.

The TSW had entrance vestibules at each end, and a saloon with conventional seating for seventy-six passengers, plus two tip-up seats and space for a wheelchair. There was a standard toilet at the end coupled to the DTS, while that at the inner end was accessible for a passenger in a wheelchair. Vehicle weight was 35.36 tonnes.

How the Class 442s might have looked – a very early impression from the mid-1980s. Some features were carried forward to the final design, notably the covers for the jumper cables. Also of interest is the livery, the popular – but short-lived – London and South East sector 'Jaffa Cake'. *Crécy archive*

The MBLS vehicle had a particularly complex layout. An entrance vestibule was followed by a small standard-class saloon for fourteen passengers. Immediately beyond this was a parcels and luggage area, with a corridor along the left-hand side looking towards the DTS. External access for loading was provided by a pair of double doors on each side of the vehicle. This was followed by the guard's 'office', with a single door on each side, and then another identical parcels and luggage area with double doors. In contrast to the power-operated passenger doors, all of these just described were of the manually operated swing variety, those for the guard's use opening inwards as on earlier stock. Beyond the second parcels area the corridor ran alongside a small service compartment, and then opened up into the buffet area with serving counter. Another entrance vestibule followed at the end of the vehicle, but this was used for loading buffet stores and was not normally available to passengers. There were no toilets in this vehicle, and the traction motors and associated equipment below the floor meant that it tipped the scales at 54.10 tonnes.

The layout described above represented that as originally planned, and as built on the first twelve units, numbers 2401–2412. However, there was a rethink as construction proceeded, with the then Parcels Sector deciding that such lavish provision was not required. As a result, units 2413 onwards were turned out with only a single 'van' next to the standard-class saloon, the second one being reconfigured as a seating area or 'snug' for passengers using the buffet, with a low-level balustrade separating it from the corridor, and twelve sofa-style seats around the sides. In the place of the double loading doors, two small windows were provided on each side. A curious feature of this area was a unit containing a litter bin in the centre of the wall opposite the corridor, which at first glance looked vaguely like a fireplace – 'snug' indeed! These revised arrangements were subsequently retrofitted to the earlier units, but this was not completed until early in 1989.

The TS was the nearest in layout to a standard Mark 3 vehicle, with entrance vestibules and toilets at each end, and eighty standard class seats but again, no luggage stacks. It weighed 35.26 tonnes.

Finally, the DTC was another rarity, being the only Mark 3 passenger vehicle (other than sleepers) with accommodation in compartments. At the inner end was an entrance vestibule, a toilet, and a small compartment housing a public telephone. Six first-class compartments followed, seating six passengers each three-a-side, and accessed by a side corridor on the right-hand side looking towards the driving end. Beyond this was a small standard-class saloon with seats for fourteen, followed by another entrance vestibule and the

Class 442 vehicles under construction by BREL at Derby Litchurch Lane, December 1987. This is a MBLS, in original layout with van areas either side of the central guard's office. *Brian Morrison*

Another view of Class 442s under construction, this time, a TS vehicle. *Brian Morrison*

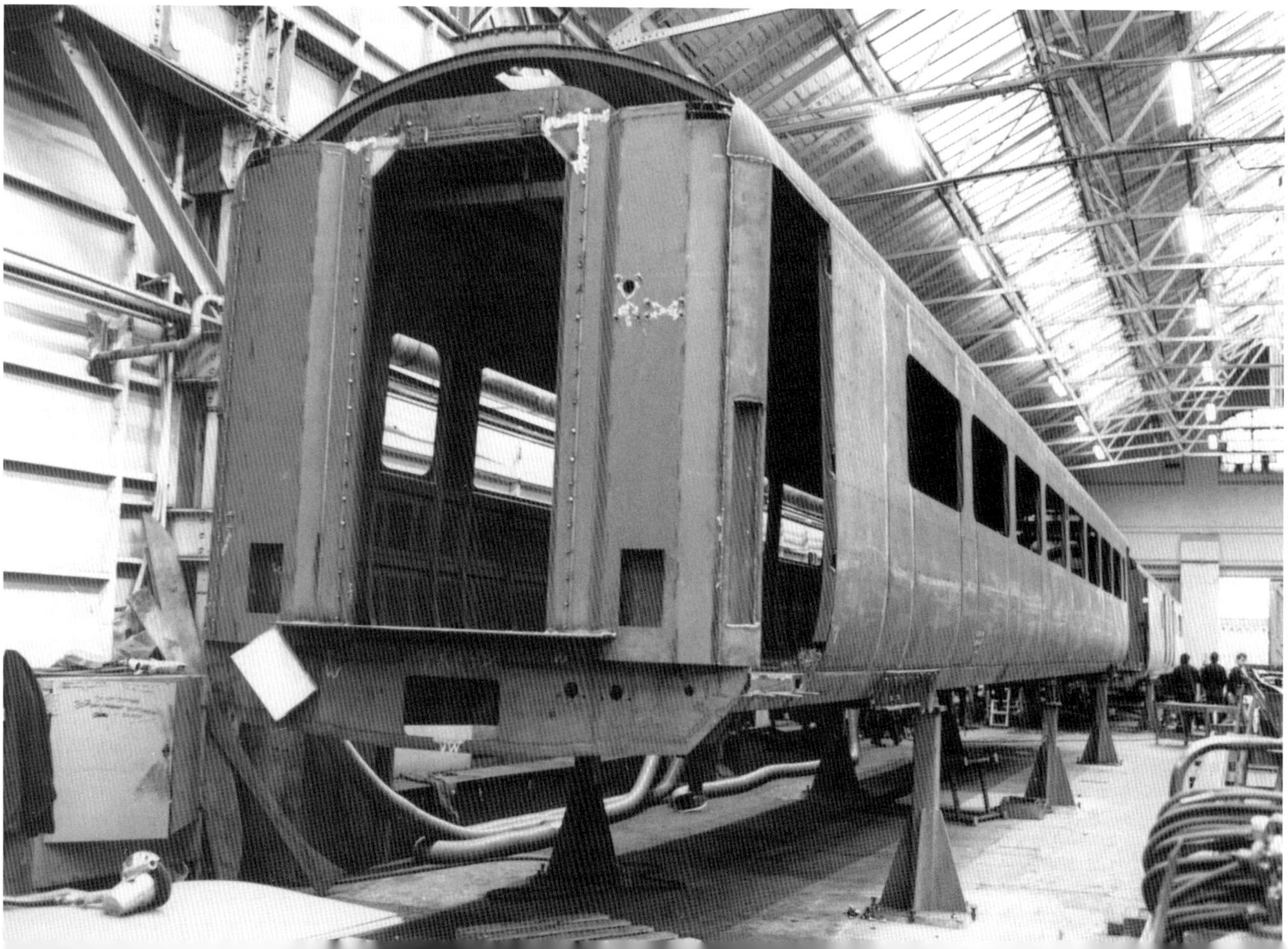

driver's cab. As in the DTS, this vestibule was not normally accessible to passengers when the cab was in use, but each cab could be closed off to provide a through passage to the gangway when units were running in multiple.

As with the MBLS, there was a rethink on the internal arrangements following initial service experience, the thirty-six first-class seats in the six compartments proving insufficient. This was resolved by simply reclassifying the fourteen standard-class seats as first, with a change in the moquette to match those in the compartments, but no alteration to the layout. New units were delivered with this alteration from 2408 upwards, the earlier sets being dealt with subsequently. This marked the first use of two-plus-two seating in open first accommodation, something now commonplace. The vehicle itself was redesignated Driving Trailer First (DTF), and like its standard-class counterpart at the other end of the unit, weighed 39.06 tonnes.

Class 442 handover, 18 December 1987. Chris Green, Network SouthEast Director, and Chris Cock, New Construction Director BREL, shake hands in front of unit 2401 at Litchurch Lane. *BREL*

Driver's desk and controls in a Class 442 unit. In spite of the twenty years that had elapsed since the introduction of the REPs, TCs and VEPs, the general layout was little changed, with three-position brake controller on the left, and forward/reverse selector and master controller on the right. The dials, from left to right, are master reservoir/brake pipe pressure, brake cylinder pressure, and speedometer. *Brian Morrison*

The 442s brought Mark 3 Inter-City standards of comfort to the Southern for the first time, as exemplified in this view of a Trailer Standard Open vehicle. Note the mix of 'airline' seats on the left, and bays around tables on the right. *BREL*

Opposite top: **Another 442 standard class interior, in this case the small fourteen-seat saloon at one end of the MBLS vehicle. The corridor on the right leads past the van area and guard's office to the buffet, while the bulkhead is adorned by an Eddie Pond mural, 'Weymouth Sands'.** *Brian Morrison*

Opposite bottom: **Most of the 442s' first-class accommodation was in comfortable six-seat compartments, as seen here. Space for coffee cups, etc, was provided both by the trinket table under the window, and the small unit between the seats nearest the camera. The murals in first class were signed 'Edward Pond'!** *BREL*

73

In terms of overall seating, a ten-car formation of two Class 442 units provided 100 first and 496 standard class seats, plus twenty-four in the 'snugs', against 108 first, 444 standard, and twenty-three in the buffet car in a 4-REP plus 8-TC formation. West of Poole, where the normal arrangements would see only a single Class 442 continuing to Weymouth, fifty first and 248 standard seats compared favourably with the forty-two first and 160 standard in a single 4-TC unit, although the 8-TC formations used at busier times obviously had the edge over a single 442.

There has been some debate about the reasons for providing compartment first-class accommodation on the 442s, and thereby complicating elements of the construction process, certainly as regards the air conditioning. It may have simply been in response to general passenger demand, but another plausible explanation is that the layout was requested by the Ministry of Defence. There were various defence and nuclear establishments around Wool in Dorset, and it was expected that service and ministry personnel would travel frequently to and from London by train. Obviously it would be much easier for them to study classified documents or have sensitive conversations in a compartment than it would in open accommodation.

Turning to the mechanical and electrical arrangements, the trailer vehicles rode on BREL T4 bogies, an updated version of a proven design already in use under other BR EMU classes. Pick-up shoes were mounted on the outer bogies of the DTS and DTF, and the inner bogies of the TSW and TS. The MBLS rode on the BREL P7 motor bogies, and here once again the old Southern 'recycling' tradition came into play. While the REP and TC units were considered life-expired, the EE546 traction motors were not, and they were reused in the 442 MBLS vehicles, which had all axles powered. The motors were apparently a very tight fit in the new bogies, and a certain amount of engineering innovation was required to accommodate them. Each five-car unit therefore had 1,600hp at its disposal, giving a total of 3,200hp – the same as for a REP plus 8-TC formation – in a ten-car train.

Most of the ancillary electrical equipment in the units was entirely 'traditional', including camshaft control equipment for the traction motors, motor generators, and compressors for the Westinghouse and EP brakes. And like the traction motors, much of it was recovered either from the REP and TC units or from other SR EMU stock. A departure from previous Southern

Opposite top: **Brand new Class 442 unit 2410 stands inside the extended Bournemouth depot on 8 April 1988. At this date, the leading coach was still configured as a composite, with a small standard-class saloon behind the driver's cab; the yellow first class stripe above the windows does not extend into this area.** *John H Bird/ANISTR.COM*

Opposite bottom: **On 14 April 1988, Class 442 units 2403 and 2401 pass Surbiton bound for Waterloo, prior to their record-breaking non-stop run to Weymouth later in the day. The headboard reads 'The Record Maker' and 'Polioplus', the name of the fund-raising campaign that benefited from the event.** *David Brown*

Below: **Among the ad hoc formations created during the introduction of the Class 442s, six 4-REP units each had one of their DMSO vehicles replaced by a Class 73 electro-diesel locomotive. Designated 3-REP, and renumbered 2901 to 2906, they could haul or propel two 4-TC units and continued to provide catering facilities, but at the expense of sixty-four standard-class seats. On 27 March 1988, 3-REP unit 2903, including locomotive 73 130, awaits departure from Eastleigh with the 13.48 Weymouth to Waterloo service. Unusually, the locomotive and 3-REP unit is at the 'country end' of the train.** *Terry Phillips*

On to Weymouth

Still a little way to go before entering scheduled passenger service, Class 442 unit 2401 passes Vauxhall with the 13.15 Waterloo to Bournemouth depot crew training trip on 21 April 1988. *Christopher J Wilson*

Named trains back on the Southern. Class 442 unit 2404 passes Beaulieu Road with the Poole portion of the up 'Royal Wessex', 06.27 Poole to Southampton, on 17 May 1988. At Southampton, the following 06.04 from Weymouth would attach, and the combined train would then call only at Southampton Parkway, Winchester, and Waterloo. *David C Warwick*

practice was the fitting of an inverter, to convert the DC traction supply to alternating current at 415 and 110v for the various auxiliary services on board, air conditioning in particular. For control purposes, the standard Southern twenty-seven wire system was used, and the units could couple to and work in multiple with Class 33/1 and 73 locomotives, and theoretically all Southern EMUs from 1951 stock onwards, although they rarely did in practice.

The overlap period during 442 introduction and REP/TC withdrawal called for some particularly innovative arrangements in respect of the traction motors, described further below, but it also caused problems elsewhere. The drivers' brake controllers were 'recycled', and once those initially available from the REPs and TCs had been exhausted, some of the new units entered service with older, five-position controllers from withdrawn 2-HAP units, which were only replaced once further REPs and TCs had been taken out of service.

The contract to supply the 442s was awarded to BREL's Litchurch Lane Works in Derby, where construction and fitting out started in late 1986 and continued through the following year and into 1988. The first completed unit, 2401, was handed over to Network SouthEast Director, Chris Green, in a ceremony on 18 December 1987.

The fifteen 4-REP units between them had 120 EE 546 traction motors. Ninety-six of these were required for the twenty-four Class 442 units, and so it was inevitable that many of the REPs would have to be taken out of service before the 442s were commissioned. This resulted in the formation of some fascinating and innovative train formations during the transitional period. The first of these were seven 4-TCB units, numbered 2801–2807, which were formed between November 1986 and June 1987. These were essentially 4-TC units with the trailer first replaced by a buffet car from a withdrawn REP. It was planned that these would work in eight-car formations with a standard 4-TC, power being provided by a Class 73 locomotive. They would be deployed primarily on the semi-fast services, and the inclusion of the former REP buffet car ensured continuity of catering facilities. One downside was the lack of any first-class accommodation in the TCB unit, meaning that an eight-car formation had only forty-two first-class seats, against eighty-four in a standard 8-TC consist. An attempt was made to address this problem in the last two units, 2806/7, by replacing the trailer brake standard with a trailer brake first from a withdrawn REP, but this was subsequently reversed in 2806, leaving 2807 as a unique TCB with twenty-four first-class seats.

Another ad hoc formation, this time 5-TCB unit 2806, departs from Southampton with the 15.53 Weymouth to Waterloo service on 4 June 1988. The 5-TCBs were essentially 4-TC units with the addition of a REP buffet car, seen here in the centre of the formation. They normally worked with another 4-TC as a nine-car train, and were frequently double-headed by a pair of Class 73 locomotives. On this occasion, 73 103 and 73 132 provided power, while 4-TC unit 8010 brought up the rear. *Terry Phillips*

There is no denying that the Class 442s were good-looking units, especially in Network SouthEast livery and with the original jumper cable covers in place. This view at Totton on 11 June 1988 displays units 2404/3 to advantage, passing with the 13.45 Waterloo to Poole service. *Christopher J Wilson*

This view at Clapham Junction on 3 August 1988 shows MBLS vehicle 62940 of unit 2404 in original condition, with van space either side of the guard's 'office'. The subsequent conversion work saw the far van, next to the buffet counter, converted to a 'snug' seating area. *Christopher J Wilson*

In anticipation of these formations entering service, and recognising the lower power to weight ratio – compared with a 4-REP – resulting from the 1,600hp Class 73s hauling or propelling eight coaches, 7 minutes was added to the semi-fast Waterloo to Bournemouth schedules in the timetable effective from 26 September 1986.

The TCB units operated through most of 1987, but the presence of blue asbestos insulation in six of the buffet cars led to the affected vehicles being withdrawn and, with the exception of 2807, the remaining vehicles were re-formed into further temporary units.

Their next incarnation was as 4-TCT units 8101–8106. In these, the buffet cars were replaced by a trailer corridor first, as in the original formation. However, these vehicles were modified at Eastleigh, the centremost compartment (of seven) being adapted as a base for a catering trolley. The remaining six compartments provided thirty-six first-class seats. These units had a relatively short life in this configuration, all but 8106 being disbanded around April/May 1988, with many of the vehicles finding further use as described below.

The fast services remained in the hands of the remaining REP/TC combinations until late in 1987, but it then became necessary to start recovering traction equipment from further REPs. The resulting shortfall was addressed by the formation of six 3-REP units, numbered 2901 to 2906, in which one of the motor coaches was removed and replaced by a Class 73 locomotive – a modification that had been anticipated in the original design specification back in 1965. Coupled to one or two 4-TC units, this gave a formation as close as possible to the original REP/TC consists, and with the same installed power as well, but with the loss of the sixty-four seats in the former motor coach. The buffet cars were six of the seven remaining asbestos-free examples, the seventh continuing to run in TCB unit 2807. Locomotives were not dedicated to specific units, but were changed over as necessary for maintenance purposes. One problem with these formations was that, whereas the original REP units had power circuits throughout ensuring that pick-up shoes at one end could feed motors at the other when passing over conductor rail gaps, there was no such connection between the remaining motor coach and the locomotive. This meant that each vehicle could sometimes be 'gapped' while the other was still drawing current, and the author remembers some 'rough' starts from Waterloo, with tremendous 'snatching' of the vehicles when this occurred.

These units remained in service until April/May 1988, when they were disbanded, the six motor coaches and three of the buffet cars being used to create three 'reconstituted' 4-REPs (2001/3/7), while the remaining vehicles (and TCB unit 2807) were re-formed with others to create yet another variation, four 5-TCB units numbered 2804-2807. These were essentially TCT units with the buffet car added back, rendering the 'trolley compartment' in the trailer corridor first redundant. They generally ran in multiple with a standard 4-TC as nine-coach trains, frequently double-headed by pairs of Class 73 locomotives. Additionally, one of the earlier 4-TCT units was made up to a 5-TCT by the addition of a second trailer corridor first, which was downgraded to standard class. It therefore continued to carry a catering trolley in the trailer corridor first, this formation arising because there were no further buffet cars available.

These units, together with a further pair of 5-TCBs formed later (2808/9), continued in service for most of 1988, with some lasting until early the following year, by which time most of the Class 442s were in service. There were a few other ad hoc formations in the meantime as well, the whole process being a tribute to the operating and maintenance staff for getting the most out of a dwindling fleet of coaches in order to keep the intensive service running. This was not quite the end for the REP and TC vehicles, however, some of which had yet further service ahead of them, as described later.

On 14 April 1988, a special record-breaking non-stop run was attempted between Waterloo and Weymouth, in conjunction with Rotary International's 'PolioPlus' fund-raising campaign. Members of the public were invited to estimate the journey time in return for donations, with prizes of holiday breaks and first-class tickets offered for the thirty-two 'nearest' estimates. Units 2401 and 2403 were used, the latter still not complete at this point, with seats missing from some vehicles. Speed limits were eased on parts of the route, notably between Farnborough and Basingstoke and Worting Junction and Winchester, where the train was allowed to run at up to 110mph. The 'single-unit' restriction west of Branksome was also relaxed. Good coordination with signalling staff was ensured by two-way communication between them and the train, with a mobile telephone link set up in the small standard-class saloon behind the cab in 2401, the unit having been turned so that the DMC vehicle was leading. In spite of a broken rail on the down fast line between Raynes Park and New Malden, resulting in a slowing to 15mph, the 142.6-mile journey was completed in just over 1 hour 59 minutes, at a start-to-stop average of 71.7mph. A maximum speed of 109mph was recorded on the long downhill stretch at 1 in 252 between Micheldever and Winchester, while other highlights were 101mph at Winchfield, and 91mph through New Milton. A total of £7,630 was raised for the charity.

Early teething problems to beset the units concerned the power door mechanisms, which were very prone to delayed opening or complete failure to open. For a period from June 1988 until January 1989 this led to the passenger door controls in the vestibules being disabled, with all door operation under the control of the guard. Remedial work involved units being taken out of service and returned to Derby for replacement of the door control units, resulting in disruption and substitution by other stock. Problems also arose with the jumper cable covers on the cab ends, causing some minor injuries to staff during coupling and uncoupling operations, and they were removed. They were replaced with a revised design a couple of years later, but in the meantime the inside of the recesses had to be painted yellow. The air-conditioning in the compartments of the DTF was not without its problems either, primarily occurring when the compartment doors into the corridor were left open. This allowed air from the compartments to bypass the temperature sensors, the solution involving the fitting of aspirator fans in the compartments to divert air back across these sensors.

As built, the units had conventional toilets that discharged on to the track. It was not BR policy at the time to fit retention toilets as standard, except on sleeping cars (to avoid track contamination at terminal stations), and on the Class 319 units for operation through the Thameslink tunnels. However, after a short time in service, staff at Bournemouth depot noticed that toilet waste contamination on bogies and underframes was worse than it had been on the REP and TC units, possibly as a result of aerodynamic effects. There had also been complaints from passengers of unpleasant odours entering through the air-conditioning. Medical analysis of the contamination indicated that it could be harmful, and staff threatened industrial action unless plans were put in place to deal with the issue. Retention tanks were therefore fitted to the units during their first C4 overhauls at Eastleigh, commencing in late 1989. Bournemouth depot was provided with a toilet 'apron' to facilitate emptying of the retention tanks, this also enabling it to service Mark 3 sleeping cars.

The timetable effective from 16 May 1988 was built around the new rolling stock, although it would be some months before the whole fleet was in service (only four units – 2404 to 2407 – being available at the outset), and footnotes advised passengers that there would be a need to change trains at Bournemouth on some services during the transition period. The new service pattern was based largely on what had gone before, but there were some significant changes as well, notably the addition of a Brockenhurst call in the Weymouth services, and the extension of the semi-fasts from Bournemouth to Poole. The higher speeds now possible translated into some journey time reductions, while the fast Weymouth services returned to their traditional xx.30 departure slot from Waterloo. In detail, the timetable was as follows:

xx.06 – Clapham Junction, Surbiton, Woking and all stations to Basingstoke (58 minutes).

xx.30 – Southampton Parkway (59 minutes), Southampton (67 minutes), Brockenhurst (82 minutes), Bournemouth (98 minutes), Poole (108 minutes), Wareham (119 minutes), Wool (127 minutes), Moreton (132 minutes), Dorchester South (140 minutes), Upwey (146 minutes) and Weymouth (150 minutes).

xx.36 – Clapham Junction, Surbiton, Woking and all stations to Southampton (112 minutes).

xx.45 – Clapham Junction, Woking (25 minutes), Basingstoke (45 minutes), Winchester (62 minutes), Eastleigh (70 minutes), Southampton Parkway (75 minutes), Southampton (82 minutes), Totton (89 minutes), Brockenhurst (100 minutes), then New Milton, Christchurch and all stations to Bournemouth (123 minutes), Branksome, Parkstone and Poole (138 minutes).

The original stopping service all the way to Bournemouth was now effectively split in two, with the xx.36 from Waterloo terminating at Southampton. A second stopper started from Southampton at xx.25 and called at all stations to Wareham, (including Holton Heath, which regained the off-peak service it had lost twenty-three years earlier). It waited at Brockenhurst for 10 minutes to be overtaken by the xx.30 from Waterloo, providing a handy connection into and out of it. The one downside to this arrangement was that the Wareham service left Southampton 3 minutes before the slow from London arrived. This meant that someone making a journey from, say, Swaythling to Millbrook, which was previously direct in 26 minutes, now had to change at Southampton and wait the best part of an hour for the onward connection. However, such an itinerary was probably fairly uncommon in the overall scheme of things, and the planners presumably decided it was a reasonable price to pay for improved connectivity generally.

A half-hourly service now operated on the Lymington branch, with trains connecting out of both the Weymouth and Poole services at Brockenhurst. By travelling on the xx.30 from Waterloo, it was possible to get from the capital to Lymington Pier in 95 minutes, a full half-hour quicker than ever before.

Before turning to the evening peak service, a couple of morning 'oddities' are worth comment. An 08.15 departure from Waterloo resurrected the name, 'Royal Wessex', and called at Winchester (54 minutes), Southampton Parkway (63 minutes), Southampton (71 minutes), Bournemouth (98 minutes), Poole (108 minutes), Wareham (119 minutes), Dorchester South (135 minutes) and Weymouth (143 minutes), giving an average speed of a shade under 60mph all the way. The second one was a summer-only (25 July to 9 September) service starting from Barnes at 08.27, and calling at Woking, Farnborough, Fleet, Basingstoke, Winchester, Southampton, Brockenhurst, Bournemouth and Poole, where it arrived at 11.13, allowing day-trippers from south-west London to be at the coast in a little under 3 hours.

The first evening variation – more correctly a 'shoulder peak' service – was the 15.45, which ran through to Weymouth, arriving at 18.52. The second down train of the day to carry the 'Royal Wessex' title was the 17.15, which ran non-stop to Winchester in 55 minutes, then called at Southampton Parkway (64 minutes), and Southampton (71 minutes) where it divided. The front portion went forward to Bournemouth (97 minutes), Poole (118 minutes), Wareham and then all stations to Weymouth (151 minutes). The rear part left Southampton 3 minutes behind and called at Totton (80 minutes), Brockenhurst (90 minutes), and all stations to Wareham (148 minutes).

The fast and semi-fast 'slots' then swapped places, with the 17.30 running to Bournemouth in 125 minutes, calling at Woking, Basingstoke, Micheldever, Winchester, Southampton Parkway, Southampton, Brockenhurst and all stations, while the 17.45 ran in its standard times to Brockenhurst, then Bournemouth (116 minutes) and all stations except Holton Heath to Weymouth (176 minutes).

On Fridays only, a 17.58 departure called at Basingstoke (43 minutes), Winchester (62 minutes), Eastleigh (69 minutes), Southampton Parkway (74 minutes), Southampton (81 minutes),

Weekend diversions for engineering work sometimes saw Class 442 units diesel-hauled between Basingstoke and Southampton via the Laverstock loop at Salisbury. On Sunday 27 November 1988, the honours fell to Railfreight-liveried Class 33/0, 33 053, leading unit 2412 away from Laverstock South Junction with the 13.45 Waterloo to Weymouth service. *G F Gillham*

Brockenhurst (97 minutes), New Milton, Christchurch and all stations to Poole (134 minutes).

The 18.30 called additionally at Winchester in 55 minutes, then ran as normal to Weymouth. The 19.30 made the standard calls and was the last 'fast' service down, while the 20.45 was extended to Weymouth to give it its last through service of the day (the 22.52 mail train and the balancing up working being withdrawn with effect from 13 May), arriving at 23.46. Poole services followed at 21.45 and 22.45, the former being the last of the day with a buffet service. These were followed by a 23.45 to Bournemouth, arriving there at 01.59, this train also detaching a portion for Salisbury at Basingstoke.

Inter-regional services continued to work through to Poole from various originating points, such as Manchester Piccadilly, Liverpool Lime Street, Wolverhampton and Glasgow Central. These included a sleeper service from Edinburgh, departing at 21.50 and arriving at Poole at 08.18 the following morning.

The Saturday service largely followed the weekday off-peak pattern, although there were some 'extras' including an 11.04 Waterloo to Wareham, which ran non-stop to Southampton in 75 minutes, and an 11.32 Waterloo to Bournemouth, non-stop to Winchester in 65 minutes. The last train to provide a buffet service was an hour earlier, at 20.45, while the 23.45 Bournemouth service was extended to Weymouth, arriving there at 03.07. Nine inter-regional services ran under the 'InterCity Holidaymaker' branding, two to Weymouth and the rest to Poole, from places as far afield as Bolton, Sheffield, Liverpool, Manchester and Aberdeen.

On Sundays, the 'fast' services ran only at 08.30, 09.30, and from 16.30 to 19.30, and they made an additional call at Basingstoke. On the hours when they didn't run, the xx.45 semi-fast services ran through to Weymouth, taking 189 minutes. Buffet service was provided on all Waterloo departures from the 08.30 to the 20.45, though only as far as Bournemouth on some services.

A striking evening shot of Class 442 units 2405/14 at Southampton Central on 20 January 1989, awaiting departure with the 15.53 Weymouth to Waterloo service. The minuscule and short-lived destination indicator above the gangway door can just be seen – you can't read it in the photograph, and you would probably have struggled if you were on the platform! *Christopher J Wilson*

The stopping services followed the pattern that had been in force broadly since 1979. A train left Waterloo for Basingstoke at xx.54, calling at Clapham Junction, Wimbledon, Surbiton, Woking and all stations, taking 73 minutes. A second hourly service left Reading at xx.40, called all stations to Basingstoke, where it provided a connection out of the Waterloo slow service (and out of the xx.30 fast service on the hours when it ran), and then continued all stations to Portsmouth Harbour via Eastleigh and Fareham, taking 120 minutes for the whole trip. At Eastleigh, the Reading to Portsmouth service provided a 2-minute connection into a xx.51 service to Lymington Pier, calling at all stations except Southampton Parkway. Connections into and out of this service were made by the xx.45 at Southampton. As an interesting comparison with the 174-minute slow service from Waterloo in 1967, if – for some obscure reason – you had wanted to travel all the way from Waterloo to Bournemouth on stopping trains on a Sunday in 1988, it would have taken you 243 minutes, with three changes!

Just three southbound inter-regional trains ran on Sundays, from Manchester Piccadilly, Liverpool Lime Street, and Newcastle.

In the up direction, the Monday to Friday off-peak pattern was as follows:

xx.02 from Wareham, calling at all stations to Southampton (88 minutes);

xx.24 from Southampton, all stations to Woking (76 minutes), then Surbiton, Clapham Junction and Waterloo (109 minutes);

xx.39 from Basingstoke, providing the alternate half-hourly service to the Southampton slow, and making the same calls to London;

xx.46 from Poole, all stations except Hinton Admiral and Sway to Brockenhurst (38 minutes), then Totton (48 minutes), Southampton (53 minutes), Southampton Parkway (63 minutes), Eastleigh (67 minutes), Winchester (77 minutes), Basingstoke (93 minutes), Woking (112 minutes), Clapham Junction (131 minutes) and Waterloo (138 minutes);

xx.53 from Weymouth, all stations except Holton Heath and Hamworthy to Poole (41 minutes), Bournemouth (51 minutes, plus a 4-minute allowance for attachment), Brockenhurst (69 minutes), Southampton (84 minutes), Southampton Parkway (93 minutes) and Waterloo (152 minutes).

The up Weymouth service overtook the Wareham starter at Brockenhurst, providing connections into and out of it there.

It also connected into the xx.24 slow Waterloo service at Southampton. A further connection was provided at Southampton out of the Wareham service into the up Poole. As in the down direction, the two stopping services 'missed' each other by 6 minutes at Southampton, meaning a lengthy wait for anyone travelling from minor stations west of the city to those on the east. The Lymington branch shuttles connected into the up Weymouth and Poole services at Brockenhurst, with a journey time to London of 105 minutes via the former.

In respect of the up peak services, an interesting comparison can be made between the first arrivals in London possible with the start of electric services in 1967, and those in 1988, as below:

Basingstoke – 07.03 (05.12 from Southampton), 4 minutes later;

Southampton, Eastleigh and Winchester – 07.03 (05.12 from Southampton), 56 minutes earlier;

Poole, Bournemouth and Brockenhurst – 07.20 (05.15 from Poole), 60 minutes earlier from Bournemouth and Brockenhurst, and 102 minutes earlier from Poole;

Weymouth – 08.48 (06.04 from Weymouth), 36 minutes earlier, but with a departure from Weymouth just 14 minutes earlier.

The highlight of the morning peak service was the up 'Royal Wessex'. One portion of this train left Poole at 06.27, and called all stations to Brockenhurst, then Totton and Southampton, arriving at 07.23. The other portion started from Weymouth at 06.04, and called at all stations except Parkstone and Branksome to Bournemouth, then fast to Southampton, where it arrived at 07.30 and attached to the Poole portion. The combined train then left at 07.33, and made calls at Southampton Parkway and Winchester, before running non-stop to Waterloo in 58 minutes.

Five inter-regional services left Poole during the day, including the return sleeper working to Edinburgh.

Saturday and Sunday services were largely a mirror image of the down pattern, the only minor exception being that on Saturdays, the 10.02 Wareham to Southampton service started back from Weymouth at 09.32.

The service pattern required twenty Class 442 units in service on Mondays to Thursdays, and twenty-one on Fridays and summer Saturdays, necessitating an availability of around 85 per cent.

The Queen travelled to Southampton in a Class 442 during the summer. She made the journey in first class on board the 15.30 ex Waterloo – although she also viewed the standard-class accommodation and the telephone booth – and was served afternoon tea by a Royal Train steward during the journey. The new units were also displayed at a number of events held during the year to commemorate the 150th anniversary of the London and South Western Railway – 'Woking 150' over the spring bank holiday, the Eastleigh Works open day on 18 September, and 'Winchfield 150' over the weekend of 25 and 26 September.

Although electrification to Weymouth eliminated the need for a traction change, the limits on train length west of Branksome meant that dividing and attaching of units at Bournemouth continued as it had in the REP/TC era. Some enhancements were evident, though, particularly the provision of buffet services on some trains through to Weymouth, which had not been possible on the TC units. In addition, many ten-car formations ran with the buffets open in each unit, and sometimes a trolley service as well, so the days of passengers walking the length of the train to seek refreshments were well and truly over.

The late delivery of some units and temporary withdrawals of others continued to see the use of ad hoc formations and units loaned from elsewhere late in 1988, with Kent Coast 4-CEP units being occasional performers. On 12 October, the 08.45 Waterloo to Poole was formed of 4-REP 2007 and newly refurbished 4-VEP 3428. With 4,200hp at its disposal, this super-powered pair produced some lively running, leaving Southampton 2 minutes late and reaching Brockenhurst a minute early, having covered the 13½ miles in 14 minutes, including a stop at Totton. The problems were compounded by early accident damage to two 442s. Unit 2417 ran into a cement mixer that had been placed on the line near Branksome on Sunday, 11 December 1988, coincidentally the day before the major accident at Clapham Junction, described in a later chapter. The damage to the unit was significant, putting it out of service for many months. Unit 2411 suffered less serious damage in a side-swipe at Wimbledon on 28 November.

The remaining REP and TC vehicles were gradually withdrawn, though not before yet more interesting re-formations had taken place. In late 1988/early 1989 two 'hybrid' 4-REPs were formed, comprising a pair of DMSO vehicles flanking an ex 4-TC TBSK and TFK, the latter having one compartment downgraded to standard class, and so reclassified as a TCK (trailer composite). These units were numbered 1901/2, repainted in Network SouthEast livery, and were intended to provide additional capacity on peak-hour services, working with remaining TC units. They stayed in service until early 1990 when, in anticipation of the South Hampshire electrification, the four DMSO vehicles and further surplus ex TC coaches were formed into four 6-REP units, numbered 1903–6. Initially, each of these had the DMSO at one end, an ex TC DTSO at the other, and two each TBSK and TCK (downgraded from TFK) in between. This formation was short-lived, however, with the units being re-formed with the motor coach in the centre – replacing one of the TCK vehicles – and an ex TC DTSO at each end, thus increasing the amount of standard-class accommodation. These changes were carried out between September 1990 and July 1991, and the units further renumbered as 1901–4. In both incarnations, the DTSO vehicles were fitted with pick-up shoes, and modifications were made to the ETH cables to provide power circuits throughout the unit, as on the 4-REPs. Although an innovative use of the remaining vehicles, reliability was poor and there was a lack of crew familiarity, and they had all been withdrawn by February 1992.

The 4-TC units 410 and 417 were retained and given a major internal refurbishment, including fitted carpets throughout and tables to each seating bay, to form the Network SouthEast 'Premier Charter' train. This was available to customers for a variety of business or private events, such as conferences, corporate hospitality, and weddings. Typical charter fees were Victoria to Brighton (single unit seating 178 passengers) for £4,000, or Waterloo to Southampton Docks (eight-coach train seating 300 passengers) for £12,000, although catering would be charged in addition to the charter fee. Another eight vehicles went to London Underground for use on other charter work, acquiring a version of Metropolitan Railway livery in the process, while a further six went to Eurostar to form a test train in connection with the Class 373 Channel Tunnel stock.

By late 1989, all of the 442s were in service and reliability was improving. Although the REPs had regularly put up storming performances over this line, the 442s were the first Southern EMUs officially authorised for 100mph running, and with long stretches of the route now cleared for this speed, the new timetables reflected this with moderate reductions in journey times, and greatly improved connectivity. The 442s also allowed Southern travellers to enjoy for the first time the air-conditioned Mark 3 comfort that had been the norm on other regions for ten years or more. They were undoubtedly a major improvement over the REPs and TCs, and passenger satisfaction levels improved as they settled into reliable operation. As the conclusion to a Network SouthEast post-implementation report of July 1989 succinctly put it, 'We have successfully set new standards for third rail express multiple-units.' However, amongst all this positivity, there was one particularly dark episode, which we shall look at in the next chapter.

Although the changeover from electric to diesel traction at Bournemouth ended with the Weymouth electrification, trains still routinely attached and divided there because the power supply limitations restricted workings further west to a single five-car unit. On 30 April 1989, unit 2416 has arrived as the 14.02 Weymouth to Waterloo, and is waiting for 2406, which has emerged from the carriage sidings, to attach. *Roland Groom*

7
Clapham

4-REP unit 2003 was the leading unit of the Poole train involved in the Clapham Junction accident, with only its rear DMSO, S62145, surviving. In happier times, 2003 is seen after arrival at Waterloo with the 12.46 from Poole on 17 August 1988. The rest of the train comprises 4-TC units 8019, nearest the camera, and 8027, out of view. *Terry Phillips*

At about 08.10 on Monday, 12 December 1988, just south of Clapham Junction, the 06.14 Poole to Waterloo service, formed 4-REP/8-TC, ran into the back of the stationary 12-VEP 07.18 service from Basingstoke. Seconds later, an empty working from Waterloo to Haslemere, formed 8-VEP, ran into wreckage from the first impact that had spread across the down fast line. The Poole train had been travelling at a speed estimated at between 35 and 40mph at the time of the collision, which was very destructive. Thirty-five people lost their lives, and a further 500 were injured, sixty-nine of them seriously enough to be detained in hospital. In terms of fatalities, it was the worst railway accident to occur in Britain for more than twenty years.

The emergency services were on the scene within around 10 minutes, and a major rescue and recovery operation got under way that continued for the rest of the day and through the night. The last of the injured were removed by 13.04, and the last bodies of those who had died by 15.45, but work to clear the wreckage and reopen the line took considerably longer. In the meantime, Network SouthEast mounted a major operation to deal with the disruption, terminating London-bound trains at Wimbledon, Woking and Basingstoke, and diverting some services via Chertsey and Staines. Central Section services to and from Victoria were still able to serve Clapham Junction, as were Windsor Line services from Waterloo, and replacement bus services were set up as soon as the emergency services no longer required access to all the surrounding roads. Once the immediate aftermath had been dealt with, investigations began and, in view of the severity of the accident, the Secretary of State for Transport, Paul Channon, directed that a full public inquiry would be held. Anthony Hidden QC was appointed to lead it.

As the evidence was gathered and pieced together, a picture of what had happened gradually emerged. The Basingstoke train had been running on the up fast line under clear signals between Earlsfield and Clapham Junction, where it was not scheduled to stop. Approaching signal WF 138, the driver was surprised to see the aspect 'step back' from green to red. Initially he made a full emergency brake application, but on seeing the line ahead to be clear, he moderated his braking and allowed the train to run slowly on to the next signal, WF 47, which was immediately south of Clapham Junction station. This signal was displaying a single yellow aspect, but he stopped his train just in rear of it and got down from his cab to report what he had seen to the signaller via the signal post telephone.

The stock to form the 06.14 from Poole was stabled overnight at Bournemouth depot, and in the normal course of events would have run empty from there to Poole prior to working the service. However, an act of vandalism on the Sunday evening prior to the accident meant that the line was blocked west of Branksome, and so the service started from that station at 06.21. Its last scheduled call before Waterloo was at Basingstoke, which it left on time at 07.38, and its journey from there was uneventful. Just after eight o'clock it passed Earlsfield and entered the cutting towards Clapham Junction, running under clear signals at between 50 and 60mph, a perfectly normal speed for this part of the journey.

The Waterloo Area Resignalling Scheme, or 'WARS', was in progress at the time. This was a major project, which had started in 1984 and was not completed until 1990. Under it, the lines from Waterloo to Putney, Kingston, Surbiton, Chessington South and Leatherhead were brought under the control of a new signalling centre at Wimbledon, and ten existing signal boxes closed. The scheme also involved the replacement of existing signalling equipment, some of it dating back to 1936. As with most schemes of this scale, much of the work was carried out at weekends, and two particular items of work carried out on Sunday, 11 December – the day before the accident – and Sunday, 27 November – two weeks earlier – were central to what happened on that Monday morning.

The work on 27 November involved some rewiring in the relay room at Clapham Junction 'A' signal box, to allow the commissioning of the new signal WF 138, replacing an existing one numbered WA 25. The work was not particularly complex, involving simply the disconnection of a redundant wire, and its replacement by new connections to the relays repeating two track circuits designated DL and DM, which were both ahead of signal WF 138 out on the line. However, the redundant wire was not removed completely, but was simply disconnected at the relay end, and pushed back out of the way.

On 11 December, the work involved the physical movement of another relay alongside one of those connected up two weeks earlier. In the course of this work, the redundant wire was inadvertently moved, and its loose end came into contact with a terminal on one of the relays controlling signal WF 138. This created a 'false feed' with the result that, whereas the signal should have returned to red as soon as a train occupied track circuit DL, immediately beyond it, it actually continued to show a 'proceed' aspect. It would only return to red once a train occupied the second track circuit, DM, a few hundred yards ahead, and beyond the following signal, WF 47. This meant that any train standing within this track circuit – as the Basingstoke train was while the driver was talking to the signaller on the telephone – was completely unprotected.

Following the weekend work, the line was reopened between 04.00 and 05.00 on the Monday morning, and the normal rush-hour traffic began to build up. Twenty-nine trains were scheduled to pass along the up fast line at this point during the 2 hours from 06.10 to 08.10, seventeen during the first 90 minutes, and twelve in the final half-hour. Drivers of some of these trains subsequently reported seeing 'odd' signal aspects, such as various signals between Earlsfield and Clapham Junction 'stepping back' from green to double or single yellow as they approached, but most dismissed this as probably resulting from the signaller resetting the route from the main to the loop platform at Clapham Junction. Whilst not entirely normal, it was not unknown for signals to change to a more restrictive aspect, and did not necessarily indicate a fault that needed reporting. The inquiry found no reason to criticise the actions of any of these drivers for failing to report what they had seen at the time, not least because the indications in the signal box were normal throughout this period, and it was highly unlikely that the fault would have been identified in time to prevent the accident. Indeed, even when a report was finally made, by the driver of the Basingstoke train after WF 138 had gone back to red as he approached it, the signaller responded – accurately – that nothing appeared to be wrong.

When the Poole train approached WF 138, it is certain that this signal was displaying a green aspect, even though the Basingstoke train was stationary a few hundred yards ahead. The driver continued, coasting with the power off, letting the speed gradually fall in readiness for the 40mph speed limit through Clapham Junction. The line is on a gentle left-hand curve at this point, and runs in a cutting, so forward visibility is limited to a few hundred yards. One can only imagine what must have gone through this poor man's mind when the rear of the Basingstoke train came into view, completely stationary on the line ahead. What is clear is that he reacted promptly; witnesses on the train and subsequent examination of the wreckage confirmed that he made a full emergency brake application. Tragically, there was simply not enough distance left for this to have any significant effect, other than reducing the train's speed by about 10mph at the point of impact.

The leading DMSO of 4-REP unit 2003, S62146, was partially reconstructed in number 25 siding at East Wimbledon for the public inquiry. It is seen here on 6 March 1989. *Colin J Marsden*

The driver of the Basingstoke train had just put down the signal post telephone, and was about to climb back into his cab when the collision occurred. He was slightly irritated by his inability to persuade the signaller that anything was wrong, and had told him he would make a report about the signal when he arrived at Waterloo. As he turned back towards the cab, he heard a muffled impact from some distance away, and watched the front of his train – which had the brakes on – move forward about 10 feet. Realising that an accident had occurred, he immediately called the signaller back and asked him to call the emergency services.

Mention has already been made of the empty Haslemere train on the down fast line that ran into the wreckage just after the accident occurred. The driver and guard of this train were both travelling together in the leading cab, and narrowly escaped injury as debris – including a brake handle – came flying through the offside cab window. The second coach of this train was derailed on hitting the wreckage, and the coupling between it and the leading coach broke, the latter coming to a halt by itself a couple of hundred yards further on.

A fourth train was very nearly involved in the accident as well. This was the 06.53 Waterloo to Waterloo 'roundabout' service, and its last scheduled call had been at Surbiton, where it stopped in the slow line platform. On departure, it crossed to the fast line after the Poole train had passed, and followed it towards Waterloo. On being told of the accident, the Clapham Junction signaller had placed all of his controlled signals in the area to red, including WF 47, alongside which the Basingstoke train was standing. This meant the 'rogue' signal was now showing single yellow, and the signal in rear of that, WF 142, a double yellow aspect. The driver of the 06.53 applied his brakes on sighting this signal, and so was travelling more slowly when he – to his surprise – saw the Poole train stationary on the line ahead, and was fortunately able to stop safely a short distance behind it. Having established what had happened in front, he went back to look at WF 138, now behind his train, and found it still showing a single yellow. He phoned the signaller to report this, and received a similar doubtful response to the driver of the Basingstoke train, assuring him that the signal should be displaying a red aspect. His reaction was understandably blunt. 'Red aspect be damned,' he exclaimed, 'there are three trains standing in front of it and it is still showing one yellow!'

The primary cause of the accident – the false feed caused by the stray wire – was quickly established. The underlying causes were more complex, and the inquiry was to highlight failures in working practices and understaffing that led to long hours and inadequate breaks. Work on the WARS scheme was originally planned to start in 1982, with completion scheduled for 1986. The existing equipment was becoming steadily less reliable on account of its age and deteriorating condition, and there was concern that any longer timescale would have led to costly and disruptive interim renewals just to keep the current system working. In the event, there were delays in securing financial approval, which put the start date back to 1984 and resulted in just the extended timescale that the planners had sought to avoid. As a result, much of the work was carried out on a far more 'staged' basis than had been intended, with new equipment being brought into use in a piecemeal fashion ahead of the main commissioning – signal WF 138 being a prime example. On top of this, cost constraints resulted in a smaller workforce carrying out the same amount of work, requiring significant amounts of overtime – one of the technicians involved had worked seven-day weeks continuously for the thirteen weeks prior to the accident. There were also failings in the processes for testing new work, so it was hardly surprising that, eventually, a mistake would be made and would go unnoticed until tragically revealed on that Monday morning. Of the ninety-three recommendations in Anthony Hidden's report, thirty-nine were aimed at addressing the failures that had taken place in the installation and testing of the new signalling equipment.

The other area to come under close scrutiny – following not only this but another fatal collision at Purley the following March – was the 'crashworthiness' of the Mark 1 vehicles involved in the accident. When it was first introduced in the 1950s, the Mark 1 coach was recognised as having exceptionally good crashworthiness characteristics, a view reinforced by its performance in some early accidents, especially when marshalled in mixed formations with pre-nationalisation stock. However, this reputation was to become somewhat tarnished in later years, particularly in comparison with Mark 2 and 3 vehicles, which employed much more modern construction techniques. The problem was that, while built entirely of steel, the Mark 1 structure still followed traditional conventions. The main strength of the vehicle lay in a heavy underframe, on top of which was a much lighter steel-framed and panelled superstructure. In a collision, if vehicles stayed upright and the couplings held them firmly in line, all was well. The slightest vertical displacement, however, could result in the underframe of one vehicle overriding the bodywork of its neighbour, and this is exactly what happened at Clapham.

The memorial stone erected to commemorate all those involved in the Clapham Junction accident, situated in Spencer Park just above the crash site.
Author

Under heavy braking, the leading end of the Poole train had dropped slightly, compressing its suspension. On impact with the rear of the Basingstoke train, this was translated into a 'burrowing' motion. The effect was to force the rear coach of the Basingstoke train bodily up onto the retaining wall alongside the line, while the Poole train ploughed underneath it and into the second to last coach, which was also forced partially upwards. Both of these vehicles sustained serious damage, but remained largely intact. The remaining vehicles of this train stayed in line and on the track. Some were derailed, but there was little major structural damage, although some internal doors, seats and transverse luggage racks were displaced and broken.

The effect on the first two vehicles of the Poole train – one DMSO and the TRB of unit 2003 – was catastrophic. The leading coach was completely demolished by its passage under the Basingstoke train coaches, with little remaining intact above underframe level for much of its length. The second vehicle – the buffet car – had its nearside completely destroyed, but as luck would have it the leading half of this contained the kitchen and bar area, which was not staffed on this service. Passengers were standing on the offside in the bar area and in the corridor alongside the kitchen, but the internal partitions and closed bar shutters afforded them some degree of protection. Nevertheless, it is no surprise that all thirty-five of those who died – including the driver – were travelling in these two vehicles.

The third coach of this train was the TBFK, with the luggage cage at its leading end. This came to rest under the eleventh coach of the Basingstoke train, the rear bogie of which penetrated its roof, causing serious injuries to standing passengers in the cage and corridor below. The remaining nine vehicles of the train suffered mainly superficial damage, similar to that in the Basingstoke train. Damage to the empty Haslemere train that ran into the wreckage was also not significant.

The inquiry report recognised that Mark 1 vehicles would have to remain in service for many more years, and one of its recommendations was that research should be carried out to determine ways of improving their crashworthiness, both through structural strengthening and some form of anti-override protection. Much work was done over the following years, and the main proposal to emerge was that Mark 1s should be fitted with an anti-override device known as 'cup and cone'. Essentially this entailed removing the side buffers – where fitted – from the headstocks, and replacing them with a cup-shaped receptacle on one side and a conical projection on the other. The theory was that, if the vehicles were forced together in a collision, the cones would engage with the cups and lock the underframes together, preventing one from overriding the other. The underframes themselves would be deliberately weakened at the ends, to allow a certain amount of controlled collapsing that would help to absorb collision energy – the 'crumple-zone' principle widely used in automotive construction and in modern rolling stock. The system was only moderately successful under test conditions, and it was established fairly early on that the standard buckeye couplers and Pullman gangways could prevent positive engagement of the cups and cones, the former by its design tendency to hold the vehicles apart, and the latter by a damping or shock-absorbing effect. This was to be remedied by modifying the couplers so that they sheared away in a collision, and more drastically, removing the gangways completely.

While not a completely satisfactory solution, the proposal eventually crystallised into a legal requirement in the Railway Safety Regulations 1999. This set a final withdrawal date for Mark 1 stock of 31 December 2004, and stipulated that vehicles remaining in service after 31 December 2002 should have the cup and cone modification. Of course, withdrawal was also dependent on the introduction of replacement stock, and in the event this did not take place as quickly as anticipated, with the result that derogations were granted to remove the cup and cone requirement, and to extend the final withdrawal deadline to the end of 2005. Interestingly, some of the very last workings of Mark 1 EMUs took place on the branch line between Brockenhurst and Lymington after this date, but this is jumping some way ahead, and will be covered in a later chapter.

Apart from the obvious personal tragedies for those involved and their families and friends, the Clapham accident also marked a sad end to the REPs' and TCs' careers as 'prime movers' on the Bournemouth line. In the early days of electrification, there had been some correspondence in the railway press about the perceived folly of high-speed push-pull operation (notwithstanding the extensive testing that had been carried out), and the inevitable accidents that would one day occur. In the light of these largely uninformed views there is a certain irony that, after twenty-one years without serious incident, Clapham was the only fatal accident in which these units were involved, its cause completely unconnected with push-pull operation.

8
South Hampshire

Although the lines between Eastleigh, Southampton and Portsmouth might be considered outside the scope of this book, their electrification had a major impact on service patterns and journey opportunities over the Bournemouth route, and is therefore part of the overall story. Completed in May 1990, this scheme saw the third rail extended from Eastleigh and St Denys to Fareham, and thence to Farlington and Portcreek Junctions to link up with the line between Havant and Portsmouth, a total of 61 route miles. This filled the gap that had existed between the Portsmouth and Southampton lines since 1967, and eliminated much of the remaining diesel working in Hampshire, both on normal scheduled services and during diversions. A major economic justification for the scheme, budgeted at £22 million, was that no new rolling stock would be required, with services provided instead by more efficient diagramming of existing electric units.

Work started on 28 July 1988, with a ceremony at Fareham station attended by Michael Portillo MP, Minister of State for Transport, Gordon Pettitt, SR General Manager, and Councillor Dudley Keep, Chairman of the Planning and Transportation Committee of Hampshire County Council. The party travelled from London on Class 442 unit 2413, which was propelled from Southampton to Fareham by Class 33 locomotive 33 114 *Sultan*, controlled from the leading cab of the 442. On arrival, the guests performed the now customary fitting of a gold-painted insulator, and assisted in the laying of a length of conductor rail.

Hedge End station was officially opened by the Secretary of State for Transport, Cecil Parkinson, on Wednesday, 9 May. He travelled from London on a special service formed of Class 442 unit 2402, seen here after arrival. Unfortunately, the service was delayed by around 30 minutes due to a traction fault. *Christopher J Wilson*

Some station improvements were carried out along the route, including platform lengthening where required to accommodate eight-coach trains, and a completely new station was provided at Hedge End, a growing residential area between Eastleigh and Botley. The station comprised up and own platforms of eight-coach length, linked by a wooden footbridge, and there was a small building housing the ticket office and a waiting area on the up side, where there was also parking. Land for the station was provided by Eastleigh Borough Council, and construction of the station was paid for by housing developers. Many of the new residential roads close to the station were named after steam locomotive classes and designers – though not necessarily with a Southern lineage – such as Maunsell Way, Britannia Gardens, and Peppercorn Way.

There were similar limitations on traction current supply to those on the Bournemouth to Weymouth route, with power at 11kV taken from the grid at Wymering, and fed to eight new substations supervised by the existing control room at Eastleigh. These were located at Moorgreen, Botley, Dimmocks Moor and Knowle on the line from Eastleigh, Woolston and Lower Swanwick on the line from St Denys, and then at Fareham and Portchester. One innovation was the use of a composite aluminium and steel conductor rail on the 4½-mile single-line section between Botley and Fareham. This combination was previously used for the bottom contact conductor rails on London's Docklands Light Railway (DLR), and it has superior conductive properties to the standard steel variety, steel being retained just for the contact surface, to minimise wear. Before the installation in Hampshire, two trial sections were installed near Dorchester and Weybridge, to assess the amount of wear, with satisfactory results. With hundreds of pick-up shoes passing daily, at speeds of up to 90mph, this was, after all, a very different environment from the relatively low-speed DLR. The reduction in voltage loss from the use of these rails between Botley and Fareham allowed one less substation here than would otherwise have been required, further improving the economics of the scheme.

Some services were electrically worked before the official opening, and a Class 73 and 4-TC formation had worked over the Portsmouth to Southampton section as early as 7 April 1990, as a substitute for a failed diesel unit. A gala day was held on Sunday, 6 May 1990 to formally mark the start of electric working. A special service ran between Eastleigh/Southampton and Portsmouth Harbour/Havant, with £2 tickets valid all day. Rolling stock in use comprised four 4-VEP units, two 4-CIGs, and two 2-HAPs. Other events on the day included displays of various rolling stock at Eastleigh works and at other principal stations on the route, and a firework display at Fareham. An official opening of Hedge End station took place the following Wednesday, 9 May, with Class 442 unit 2402 unit conveying Cecil Parkinson – then Secretary of State for Transport – from London. Unfortunately, this unit arrived more than 30 minutes late because of a fault, and 2409 was pressed into service to work the return trip! Some services over the route continued to be diesel worked during that week, with the full electric timetable commencing on Monday, 14 May.

This built on the 'Wessex Electrics' service of 1988, but took full advantage of the newly electrified routes to provide additional journey opportunities, and was marketed as 'Solent Link'. The centrepiece was a new Waterloo to Portsmouth Harbour via Eastleigh and Fareham service, departing Waterloo at xx.10. It called at Woking (24 minutes), Basingstoke (45 minutes), Winchester (62 minutes), Eastleigh (71 minutes, then all stations to Portsmouth and Southsea (108 minutes), and Portsmouth Harbour (112 minutes). Up services left Portsmouth Harbour at xx.52, and reached Waterloo in 114 minutes. In combination with the hourly Poole workings, this new service gave two semi-fast trains an hour on the Woking–Basingstoke–Winchester–Eastleigh axis, the first real increase in frequency on this since 1967, albeit that the intervals were not exactly even, being around 25 minutes/35 minutes in the down direction, and 20/40 going up. It also provided the best-ever through service between Fareham and London.

Some portion working was introduced in the evening peak period. The 17.30 Waterloo to Bournemouth now detached a portion at Eastleigh for Fareham, arriving there at 19.06. The 18.00 Waterloo to Poole was replaced by a 17.56 departure for Poole and Portsmouth Harbour, which divided at Eastleigh. There was a later last train from Waterloo, at 01.05 to Southampton on Monday to Friday mornings, and to Eastleigh on Saturdays.

In the morning peak, Weymouth gained an additional departure at 06.38, combining with the existing 06.55 from Poole at Southampton, and arriving at Waterloo at 09.24. The flexibility of the catering arrangements on the Class 442 units was demonstrated by this working, with the Weymouth portion having a trolley service as far as Southampton, and the Poole portion having a buffet from Bournemouth, which then served the whole train once the attachment had been made.

There were trains to Waterloo from Portsmouth Harbour at 05.04 (132 minutes), Fareham at 06.00 (95 minutes), Portsmouth and Southsea at 06.38 (133 minutes), and Portsmouth Harbour at 07.04 (121 minutes). There was also an Eastleigh to Waterloo train in the morning peak via Fareham and the Portsmouth direct line. A shuttle service between Eastleigh and Portsmouth ran after the evening peak period, on Saturday evenings, and all day on Sundays.

Some consequential amendments were made. Exeter and Salisbury services were ousted from their former xx.10 departure slot by the new Solent Link services, and retimed to depart 5 minutes later at xx.15. The alternate Basingstoke/Southampton slow services were retimed to leave Waterloo a minute earlier, and swapped over so that the xx.05 now ran to Southampton, in place of the xx.36 previously. This gave a slightly better connection into and out of the Wareham stopping service, which – also taking advantage of the electrification between Fareham and St Denys – now ran to and from Portsmouth Harbour, calling at all stations between there and Southampton.

A through service from Lymington Pier to Waterloo ran on weekdays, departing at 06.40, calling at Brockenhurst, Totton, Southampton, all stations to Woking and then fast, taking 148 minutes in total. On Mondays to Saturdays, the hourly Victoria to Portsmouth Harbour service was diverted via Fareham and

Above: **There are signs of preparatory work for the Solent Link electrification in this view at Bursledon on 20 May 1989. New conductor rails are lying in the four foot, while cables have been laid under the westbound platform surface on the right – both platforms were later resurfaced. A Class 156 'Sprinter' unit passes with the 13.10 Portsmouth Harbour to Cardiff Central service.** *Terry Phillips*

St Denys to terminate at Southampton Central, thus providing a regular direct link between the city and Gatwick Airport. On Sundays, these trains ran into Portsmouth Harbour, but were then extended to provide the Solent Link stopping service to Southampton.

In terms of rolling stock, the new Waterloo services were worked largely by 4-CIG units during the off-peak along with some 4-VEPs. 4-BEP and 2-HAP units also put in appearances, normally on the shorter workings, which did not venture beyond Eastleigh. The recently formed 6-REP units were generally restricted to peak-hour services, especially those that involved portion working. The Portsmouth to Wareham services were generally worked by CIGs or VEPs, while CIGs were also the normal equipment on the trains from Victoria.

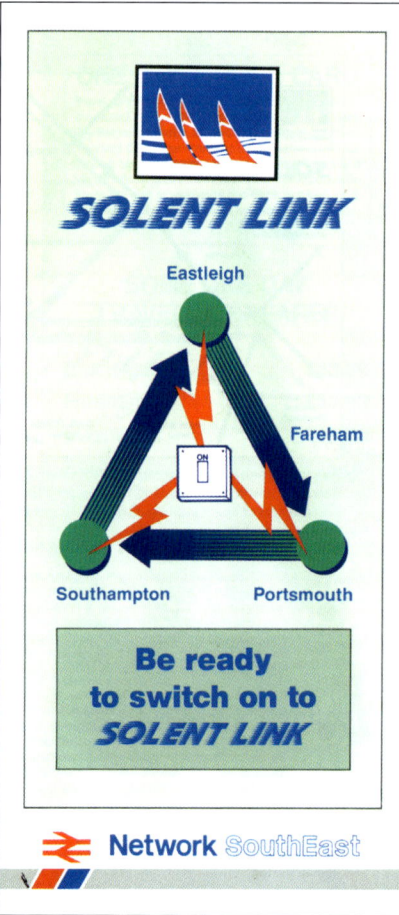

Network SouthEast publicity leaflet for the Solent Link electrification.
Terry Phillips Collection

The Solent Link electrification came into its own for diversionary purposes on the Sundays 18 and 25 November 1990, when engineering works closed the main line, and services between Waterloo, Bournemouth and Weymouth were diverted from Woking to Havant, and then via Fareham to Southampton. This was the first occasion on which 442s had run over the Portsmouth direct line, and the first time that Bournemouth line services had been diverted between Havant and Southampton without the need for diesel haulage.

The new station at Hedge End nears completion during April 1990, as Class 207 DEMU 207 010 passes with an Eastleigh to Portsmouth service. *John H Bird/ANISTR.COM*

Solent Link gala day, Sunday, 6 May 1990. Bunting adorns the red lamp posts and pristine platforms at Hedge End, while the very first train to serve the station – the 09.07 Eastleigh to Portsmouth Harbour – approaches in the distance formed of 2-HAP units 4321 and 4317. *David Phillips*

Among the various rolling stock displays to mark the Solent Link gala day, Foster Yeoman Class 59 locomotive, 59 003, *Yeoman Highlander* was stabled at Botley station. It attracts some attention here as 4-VEP unit 3017 calls with the 12.07 Eastleigh to Portsmouth Harbour service. *John H Bird/ANISTR.COM*

A band plays at Netley station as part of the Solent Link gala day celebrations, as 4-VEP unit 3046 arrives with the 12.48 Southampton to Havant service. *John H Bird/ANISTR.COM*

Two of the short-lived 6-REP units are seen here at Waterloo after arrival with the 06.00 service from Bournemouth on 18 May 1990 – unit 1906 in full view, and the end of 1903 at the left. At this date, 1906 was yet to be re-formed with the motor coach in the centre. It is at the buffer stops in this view, while the two vehicles nearest the camera are ex 4-TC driving trailers – note the new pick-up shoe beams fitted to the outer bogies. *Terry Phillips*

Another view of a 6-REP in original formation – unit 1903 is about to run empty stock from Fareham to Eastleigh after arrival with the 17.30 service from Waterloo on 27 June 1990. DMSO 62145, leading, was originally part of 4-REP 3003. The other five coaches were all former 4-TC vehicles. *Christopher J Wilson*

The 6-REPs found fairly regular use on peak-hour portion workings. On 18 July 1990, units 1906 and 1903 storm past Worting Junction with the 17.30 Waterloo to Fareham and Bournemouth service. The train will divide at Eastleigh. *Christopher J Wilson*

The 6-REPs were re-formed between September 1990 and July 1991, the motor coach being moved to the centre of the unit, with 4-TC driving trailers at each end. This view of unit 1901 at Portcreek Junction on 11 June 1991 shows the relocated motor coach, 62142. The windscreens and jumper cable apertures on the vehicle end were plated over, but the cab side windows and vestibule doors remained. *Christopher J Wilson*

Side-lit by low afternoon sun, Class 442 units pass at New Malden with up and down Bournemouth services on a July day in 1991. *Author*

Further problems befell the new stock over the weekend of 9 and 10 February the following year, when the whole fleet of 442s were taken out of service following reports of problems with axle and traction motor bearings. This caused major disruption to services, which had to be operated by a mixture of 4-CIGs, 4-VEPs, and 4-TCs powered by Class 73 locomotives.

December 1991 saw completion of major refurbishment work at Eastleigh station. The entrance was completely rebuilt, providing more space for passenger circulation, and a new refreshment area and ticket office. Lifts were installed, and a large car park was also provided, on the site formerly occupied by the up loop, which had been taken out of use during the 1980s.

9
Towards Privatisation

In the early 1990s it was recognised that the Class 442s were not being as well utilised as they might be on Bournemouth and Weymouth workings. This was not considered acceptable for some of Network SouthEast's newest – and most expensive – stock, particularly against the backdrop of a marked fall in London commuter traffic and a consequent drop in revenues. It was therefore decided to diagram the units on some Portsmouth direct line services from the May 1992 timetable change. They were already cleared for the route for diversion purposes, but driver and fitter training was required, and this entailed the transfer of some units away from the Bournemouth line from February of that year. As temporary cover, three Ramsgate-based 4-CEP units – 1588/97/1606 – were loaned to Bournemouth from 10 February until 10 May.

This timetable also saw some changes to Bournemouth services, primarily moving the Waterloo departure slot for the Poole semi-fast services back 8 minutes to xx.53. This was done to ease pathing difficulties, but also meant that passengers connecting from this service to the Lymington branch now had a 25-minute wait at Brockenhurst. Other changes reflected both increases and decreases in demand – the 09.53 Weymouth to Bournemouth service was extended to Waterloo, while the 15.03 Poole to Waterloo, 15.15 Weymouth to Waterloo, and 20.02 Wareham to Bournemouth were all withdrawn.

One of the first manifestations of the new shadow franchise was the 'South West Trains Shuttle' 20-minute interval service between Waterloo and Southampton, which was introduced with the 1994 summer timetable. On the first day – 31 May – Class 442 units stand side by side at Winchester with the 14.55 ex Southampton and the 14.10 ex Waterloo. *Author*

An open weekend at Bournemouth depot over 12–13 September was the largest event ever held there. On display from the BR fleet were ten diesel and electric locomotives and eight diesel and electric multiple-units, including the preserved 4-SUB 4732 and 2-BIL 2090. Privately owned exhibits included nine diesel and electric locomotives, and two steam locomotives, 'West Country' 34027, *Taw Valley*, and Standard Class 4 75069. The whole depot area was given over to the event, and visitors were transported to and from Bournemouth station by a shuttle service using 4-VEP units 3480 and 3521 powered by Class 33 locomotive 33 114, *Ashford 150*. In addition, a special service ran to and from Waterloo each day using Network SouthEast's 'Premier Charter' set, hauled by the National Railway Museum's preserved Class 71 locomotive, E5001.

Early 1993 saw major works carried out on the bridge between the Town and Pier stations in Lymington, with the line remaining closed until 29 March. On Saturday, 3 April, Hertfordshire Railtours operated four shuttle services between Weymouth Town and Quay, over the tramway through the town's streets, using the Network SouthEast 'Premier Charter' set hauled/propelled by Class 33 locomotive 33 109. In spite of heavy rain for most of the day, some 1,200 people travelled on the shuttles, while hundreds more turned out to watch.

The 1993 summer timetable saw both half-hourly slow services from Waterloo terminating at Basingstoke, stops at Micheldever and Shawford being picked up by the 'Solent Link' services, which left Waterloo 5 minutes earlier at xx.05. The Portsmouth to Wareham service was split into two sections – one between Portsmouth and Southampton, and the other from there through to Wareham, although this was withdrawn during the off-peak from October, leaving Millbrook, Redbridge and Holton Heath with a peak-hour only service.

In 1994 there was further development at Southampton Airport, with the opening of a new passenger terminal. The station was renamed once again, this time becoming simply 'Southampton Airport Parkway' with effect from the timetable change on 29 May. At the same time, Southampton station reverted to its pre-1967 title of 'Southampton Central'.

As a precursor to privatisation, the entire UK passenger network was divided up into 'shadow' franchises, ready to be let to incoming private operators in due course. From March 1994, the former Network SouthEast South Western Division was transferred to South West Trains, one of the first shadow franchises to be launched. External changes were minimal at first; the Network SouthEast livery remained, but some new logos and branding started to appear on rolling stock over the following months.

One of the 'losers' in the 1994 summer timetable was the Solent Link service, which was cut back to a shuttle between Portsmouth and Winchester. On 31 May, 4-CIG unit 1312 crosses to the Baltic siding at Winchester after arrival with the 13.59 service from Portsmouth. Following reversal, it will operate the 15.05 return working. *Author*

The new arrangements brought some major changes on the Bournemouth line with the May 1994 timetable. The most significant was the introduction of the 'South West Trains Shuttle', a 20-minute frequency service between Waterloo and Southampton Central in both directions. In place of the time-honoured fast to Weymouth and semi-fast to Bournemouth/Poole at roughly 30 and 45 minutes past the hour, the new pattern was as follows:

xx.10 – Farnborough (giving it a non-stop service from London in 32 minutes), Basingstoke (45 minutes), Winchester (63 minutes), Southampton Airport Parkway (72 minutes), Southampton Central (79 minutes);

xx.30 – Winchester (52 minutes, its best ever off-peak timing), Southampton Airport Parkway (62 minutes), Southampton Central (69 minutes), Brockenhurst (84 minutes), Bournemouth (100 minutes, as in 1967, but with three additional stops), Poole (110 minutes) and all stations to Weymouth (156 minutes);

xx.50 – Clapham Junction, Woking, Basingstoke, Winchester, Eastleigh, Southampton Airport Parkway, Southampton Central, Totton, Brockenhurst, Bournemouth and all stations except Sway and Hinton Admiral to Poole. This was exactly the same stopping pattern as the xx.45 of the 1988 timetable, with the same running times, give or take a minute or two.

In the up direction, trains left Southampton Central for Waterloo at the same 20-minute intervals, as under:

xx.15 (xx.50 from Weymouth);

xx.35 (xx.41 from Poole);

xx.55 Southampton Central starter.

Running times from Southampton were slightly longer than for the down services, at 73 minutes (Weymouth starter), 88 minutes (Poole starter), and 83 minutes (Southampton starter). All of these trains had catering facilities.

There was further reorganisation of other services, following from those the previous year, and some 'losers' as a result. The 1990 'Solent Link' service was cut back to run only between Portsmouth and Winchester, reversing there in the Baltic siding, north of the station. Off-peak, Micheldever was served by a two-hourly service between Reading and Portsmouth, but still had direct services to London in the mornings and evenings. Minor stations west of Southampton saw some improvement in the form of a two-hourly Southampton to Brockenhurst train, and an hourly service from there on to Poole, although the hourly Portsmouth to Southampton introduced in 1993 continued to operate. A half-hourly service continued to operate on the Lymington branch, with good connections into and out of the fast Weymouth trains, but not so good with the Poole ones.

Network SouthCentral services between Victoria and Southampton were extended to Bournemouth from 31 May 1994. On that day, 4-CIG unit 1906 pauses for custom at Brockenhurst with the 11.50 Bournemouth to Victoria service. It will take another 170 minutes to reach London, compared with around 90 for services to Waterloo! *Author*

This timetable also saw an incursion deep into South West Trains territory by the neighbouring shadow franchise, Network SouthCentral, with further extension of the hourly Victoria to Southampton service through to Bournemouth. This used the bay platform on the up side of the station – platform 1 – which was brought back into use to accommodate this working, and part of the rationale behind the extension was to reduce platform occupation at Southampton. Despite calling only at Brockenhurst on its way through the New Forest, this was an awfully long way round to reach London, but it did give travellers from Dorset a direct service every hour to Gatwick Airport.

Morning peak services on the main line were little changed from 1990, but on the South Hampshire route the first direct train to London was now the 06.30 from Fareham in place of the 05.04 from Portsmouth Harbour, although an earlier connection was available via Eastleigh. In the down direction, the 17.30 to Fareham went back 2 minutes to 17.32, and no longer detached a portion for Bournemouth, while the former Portsmouth portion of the 17.56 departure now terminated at Fareham.

The Saturday service followed the Monday to Friday off-peak pattern, although on the Poole and Weymouth trains, buffet service was only provided as far as Brockenhurst. Six northbound and five southbound inter-regional services operated. On Sundays, a completely different pattern applied. Weymouth services departed at xx.30, and called at Basingstoke (51 minutes), Winchester (68 minutes), Southampton Airport Parkway (87 minutes), Brockenhurst (103 minutes), New Milton (111 minutes), Bournemouth (121 minutes) and all stations except Holton Heath to Weymouth (180 minutes). Even allowing for the additional stops compared with the weekday service, there was quite a lot of 'slack' in these timings. The semi-fast reverted to its former departure slot at xx.45, and made the usual calls (with the addition of Micheldever and Shawford on alternate hours) to Eastleigh, where it divided. The front portion then called at all stations except Millbrook and Redbridge to Bournemouth, while the rear ran via Fareham to Portsmouth and Southsea. The Sunday walker and tourist potential of the New Forest was clearly

Solent Link diversion. Weekend resignalling work between Basingstoke and Eastleigh through the summer of 1995 saw Bournemouth and Weymouth services routed via the Portsmouth direct, Fareham and St Denys. On 26 August, a pair of Class 442 units cross the River Hamble at Bursledon with the 13.50 Waterloo to Weymouth service. *Author*

recognised here, with Lyndhurst Road and Beaulieu Road enjoying an hourly service, and a half-hourly shuttle continuing to operate between Brockenhurst and Lymington. Buffet service was only provided on the Weymouth trains.

Under-utilisation of the Class 442s was no longer a problem; in fact, with some of them still working Portsmouth direct services, these new arrangements saw them spread a little thinly. While they continued to work all of the Weymouth and Poole services, some of those to Southampton were worked by 4-CIGs, mainly those with the additional weak field 'Greyhound' modifications.

At the end of March 1995, ownership of the Weymouth Tramway passed to the local authority, meaning that their approval was needed for the operation of train services between town and quay. Previously, this had been an automatic right for British Rail. On 20 April, the 09.50 Weymouth to Waterloo service, formed of Class 442 unit 2401, ran into a pushchair that vandals had thrown on to the line near Moreton. The service was terminated and the unit later hauled by a locomotive to Bournemouth depot, where the cost of repairs was assessed at around £20,000.

The 1995 summer timetable saw the Portsmouth direct line follow the Bournemouth route with a similar 20-minute frequency service, which resulted in the 442s being spread even more thinly. The 08.15 Waterloo departure lost its 'Royal Wessex' branding, although the title was still applied to the up working and to the 17.15 down, while the 11.30 Waterloo to Weymouth gained a name as the 'Channel Island Express'.

The same year saw resignalling of the line between St Denys and Worting Junction, west of Basingstoke, in a project taking some seven months. Largely, this involved replacement of the original 3-aspect signals, installed with electrification in 1967, with 4-aspects. There was also provision for bi-directional working between Micheldever and Eastleigh, to provide more flexibility at times of disruption or during engineering work. Final commissioning took place between 18 and 26 November, with trains being hand-signalled through parts of the area.

From the start of the winter timetable on 24 September, Lyndhurst Road station was renamed Ashurst New Forest. This better reflected the station's location – being in the village of Ashurst while almost 3 miles from Lyndhurst – as well as helping to promote it as a railhead for the tourist area.

10
South West Trains

South West Trains launch day, 5 February 1996. Class 442 unit 2402 poses at Waterloo in the company's new livery, essentially the Network SouthEast scheme with an orange stripe added, to reflect the Stagecoach group's house colours. No. 2402 was the only Class 442 to wear this livery, but it was widely applied to the Mark 1 EMUs and the Class 455 suburban units. *Colin J Marsden*

The first real – as opposed to shadow – franchises were let in early 1996, with the Stagecoach Group becoming the successful bidder for South West Trains (SWT), and taking over from 4 February. Stagecoach was best known as a bus operator, with its roots in Scotland, but expanding its operations throughout the UK during the 1980s and '90s. It had previously dabbled in rail transport under the short-lived 'Stagecoach Rail' operation, which saw the company hire two Mark 2 seated coaches on Anglo–Scottish sleeper services, selling cut-price tickets for the journey. SWT, though, was its first venture into large-scale rail operation, right at the beginning of a new era for Britain's railways.

A new livery was designed, based largely on the Network SouthEast stripes for ease of application, but with the addition of an orange stripe to complete the Stagecoach group's house colours. This was applied to Class 442 unit 2402 secretly in advance, and it was 'unveiled' at Waterloo on launch day. The logo developed for the shadow franchise was retained, and carried on coach bodysides along with the wording, 'A Stagecoach Company'. The new livery gradually appeared on other rolling stock, along with new station signage and branding.

The new operation got off to a bit of a shaky start. In an early attempt to cut costs, an inaccurate reassessment of the number of drivers required resulted in many taking up a generous voluntary redundancy offer and departing. Unfortunately, it transpired that the full service could only then be provided with significant overtime working, which many drivers were not

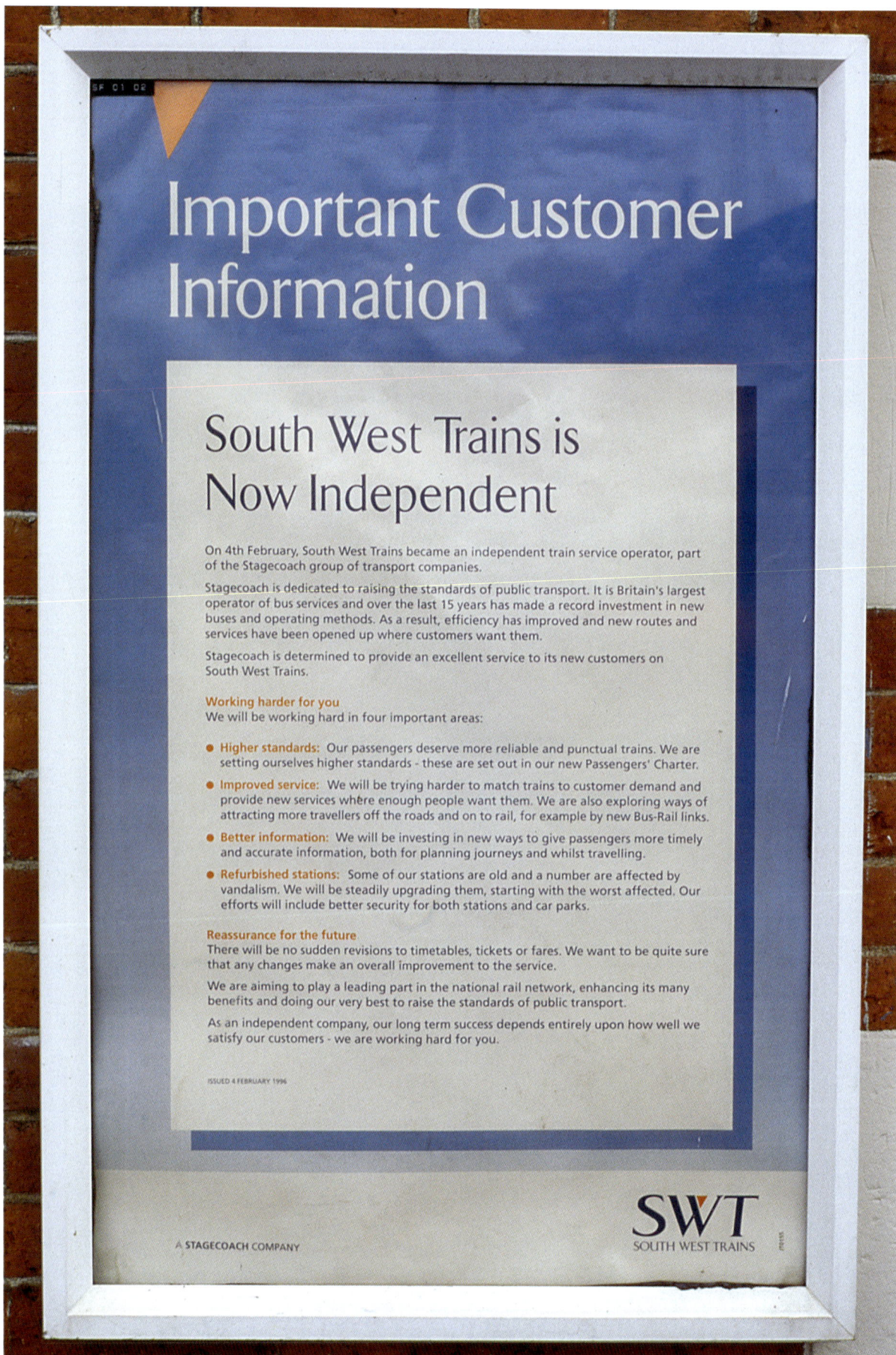

prepared to participate in. The outcome was a period of some months with widespread cancellations and alterations, causing considerable inconvenience to passengers. The position was eventually resolved by the recruitment of further drivers!

A serious landslip just south of Bincombe Tunnel resulted in single-line working over the down line between Dorchester and Weymouth, and some bus substitution. Disruption continued from the end of February to the middle of March. A slightly more amusing incident occurred on 16 April, when the 20.53 Waterloo to Poole service was incorrectly routed on to the Salisbury line at Worting Junction, and ended up 'off the juice'! The train continued its journey almost an hour and a half later, after being rescued by a diesel locomotive despatched from Eastleigh.

The 1996 summer timetable saw the restoration of direct off-peak services between Waterloo and 'Solent Link' stations, by extending one of the half-hourly Basingstoke stoppers to and from Portsmouth. Some relief was also provided for the hard-pressed 442s by extending two of the Waterloo to Southampton services – the 10.10 and 14.10 departures – to Salisbury, operated by Class 159 diesel units. There were balancing workings in the up direction, with the 11.55 and 15.55 Southampton departures starting back from Salisbury at 11.15 and 15.15 respectively. The trend for naming trains continued as well, with the 12.30 Waterloo to Weymouth and 15.48 return working acquiring the historic 'Bournemouth Belle' title on weekdays.

The company suffered further problems in August 1996 when wheel-bearing problems on 4-CIG units led to the thirty-four-strong fleet being withdrawn from service for safety reasons. Other units substituted as far as possible, including three 4-CEP units transferred from neighbouring operator Connex South Central, and others taken out of storage, but inevitably there was some significant service disruption, including cancellations. After investigation, the cause of the problem was traced to contaminated grease used in the axleboxes. This was relatively easily remedied, and most of the CIGs had returned to service by mid-September, but a heavy fine was levied on the company as a consequence.

On the positive side, one of the operator's early improvements was the introduction of bus 'feeder' services, using its own road vehicles, from Romsey to Winchester, and from Bordon to Liphook (on the Portsmouth line).

Above: **Resignalling and remodelling work at Woking over the weekend of 28/29 September 1996 saw the down lines closed, with down services working 'wrong line' over the up fast. Passing the 1937 signal box, Class 442 units 2413 and 2409 regain the down fast line south of the station with the 12.16 Waterloo to Poole service.** *Author*

Opposite: **The new regime was announced by these posters placed at stations across the network over the weekend of 3/4 February 1996.** *Author*

The new signalling centre at Woking, seen nearing completion on 24 September 1996. Architecturally, it is some way behind its 1937 'glasshouse' predecessor! Author

Resignalling work started in the Surbiton to Woking area in the latter part of the year, with a new control centre at Woking replacing the existing 1937 box there and the 1970 one at Surbiton. The work involved some layout changes, including the provision of reversible working on all lines through Woking, together with a new London end bay (platform 3) between the up and down fast lines there. Final commissioning was not until the August bank holiday weekend the following year.

In 1997 there were a number of changes that affected the route. The first was a fairly major reshuffle of Mark 1 rolling stock, with the company transferring a number of 4-VEP units to the Connex South Eastern franchise, and taking – eventually – twenty-nine 4-CEP units in return. The thinking behind this is not entirely clear; the VEPs had higher seating capacity than the CEPs, although against this the CEPs, with their low-density, two-plus-two, standard-class seating, provided a better travelling environment for longer journeys. Another factor may have been that while the VEPs were owned by lessor Angel Trains, the CEPs belonged to Porterbrook, which Stagecoach had acquired in August 1996 – better perhaps to be paying leasing charges to a company in the same corporate group. Certainly the CEPs, the oldest of which had been in service for thirty-eight years by this time, were in quite variable condition, but SWT seemed to acquire the better examples. They were allocated to Fratton depot, which looked after them very well, even getting some of them into the Stagecoach livery quite quickly, and they were to become reasonably regular performers on the Bournemouth line.

The second development involved major improvements to the facilities at Southampton Airport Parkway, with a new single-storey building on the up side containing a ticket office, waiting area, buffet, first-class lounge and toilets. A particular innovation was a completely open ticket counter, incorporating a low-level section for passengers in wheelchairs. Disabled access was not so good elsewhere, however, with the 1966 concrete footbridge remaining the only access between platforms – and to the airport terminal from the up side. It would be another thirteen years before this was remedied. In the meantime, a courtesy taxi service was provided to enable disabled passengers to get from one side to the other.

The third change was the franchising of the inter-regional services to the Virgin group, operating under the 'Cross Country' brand. Service frequency was increased, eventually becoming hourly for most of the day, while locomotive-hauled and HST formations would ultimately give way to the new Class 220 'Voyager' and Class 221 'Super Voyager' DEMUs.

In 1998, a major refurbishment programme commenced on the Class 442 fleet, which had been in service for around ten years. The work was shared between Adtranz at Crewe and Alstom at Eastleigh, and was initially expected to take eighteen months. Unit 2416 was the first to be treated, with the van area being reduced in size to increase the saloon seating to thirty. The partition between the guard's office and the van space was also removed, and stowage racks for five bicycles installed in this area.

Externally, a new livery was applied – predominantly white, relieved by blue bands along the windows and lower bodysides. The red and orange colours were formed into an 'upsweep' at each end of the unit, starting at solebar level and moving up and over the roof about a third of the way along each driving vehicle; orange 'lining' was provided along the top of the lower blue bodyside band. A new logo, formed of the name, 'South West Trains' in bold blue and orange capitals, with a dot over the 'I', was applied to the bodysides, but the 'Stagecoach Company' branding was dropped. There were suggestions that this was because of the poor publicity that accompanied the franchise's 'teething troubles' mentioned above, but the official line was that it created too long a legend for practical application on vehicle sides.

Initially, it was planned to extend the red area surrounding the cab windows across the upper half of the end gangway doors, leaving the just the bottom half in 'warning yellow'. However, concern was expressed that from a distance in bright daylight, this might mimic the red rear headcode blinds on Mark 1 units, and mislead infrastructure staff into thinking that a train was heading away from them, rather than towards them. There was thus a last-minute change of plan, and the gangway doors remained yellow for their full height.

The work carried out at Eastleigh was largely internal, involving new seat upholstery in SWT's red 'timetable pattern' moquette, new carpets, and the removal of the Eddie Pond murals from the saloon ends. Additional seating was installed in the 'snug' in the MBLS vehicles, taking capacity for this area up to seventeen, and to forty-seven for the vehicle as a whole. The opportunity was also taken to replace the troublesome covers for the multiple and brake jumpers with a new, lightweight version. Unit 2401 was the first to be outshopped, in July 1999, while the last, 2417, was not completed until March 2001.

Although the franchise agreement did not include a requirement to provide new rolling stock, SWT was conscious of the deadlines for withdrawal of Mark 1 stock, and the need to provide for growth generally, and made an early bid to acquire new trains in 1998. These took the form of thirty four-car Class 458 units from Alsthom, referred to as 'Junipers' after their traction package, and quickly acquiring the Southern designation of 4-JOP. They were 'outer-suburban' in configuration, with two-plus-three seating in standard class, small first class areas with two-plus-two seating at each end of the unit, and external sliding doors at the one third/two third positions. They had through gangways but, in an attempt to provide a 'cleaner' front end they were retractable, and concealed by flush doors across the driving ends when not in use. Unfortunately, this also meant that they required manual intervention to connect and disconnect, unlike the straightforward 'Pullman' gangways used on most stock in the UK for decades. As a result, they were little used in practice. Generally, the units proved troublesome, and after many attempts by Alsthom to remedy the numerous faults, they were taken out of service and placed in store. In spite of their 100mph capability, they were allocated to Reading line services, but did carry out some extensive high-speed test running on the Bournemouth line. They did, however, wear from delivery the new South West Trains livery first seen on the refurbished Class 442 units, though with a considerably shorter 'upsweep' at the unit ends.

May 1999 saw yet further enhancements to the Bournemouth line timetable, the main feature being an increase in the frequency between London and Southampton from three to four trains an hour, something probably undreamt of at the time of electrification! The new pattern of departures from Waterloo was as follows:

> xx.00 – Basingstoke, Winchester, Southampton Airport Parkway, Southampton Central, Brockenhurst, all stations to Wareham (142 minutes);
>
> xx.15 – Farnborough, Basingstoke, Winchester, Eastleigh, Southampton Central (81 minutes);
>
> xx.30 – Woking, Winchester, Southampton Airport Parkway, Southampton Central, Bournemouth, principal stations to Wareham and all stations to Weymouth (157 minutes);
>
> xx.45 – Clapham Junction, Woking, Basingstoke, Winchester, Eastleigh, Southampton Airport Parkway, Southampton Central, all stations to Poole (175 minutes).

The one really new service here was that on the hour to Wareham; the other three had all featured in the 1994 timetable but were retimed slightly to fit the quarter-hourly pattern. The Woking stop was inserted into the Weymouth service to connect with the 'Railair' coach service to Heathrow Airport. Given the different stopping patterns, the two faster services were only a few minutes behind the slower ones at Southampton Central, and the Poole service was overtaken twice en route, by the Wareham service at Southampton, and the Weymouth one at Brockenhurst. Thus you could catch, say, the 11.30 from Waterloo, and still reach Bournemouth or Poole ahead of the 10.45, which had a 45-minute head start from London! A similar arrangement operated in the up direction, with the Poole starter passed by the up Wareham at Brockenhurst, and the up Weymouth at Southampton Central. All of this required some fairly slick operating at Brockenhurst, as both up and down Poole services had to use the reversible up loop there, the down loop being required by the Lymington branch shuttles.

This new timetable was completely beyond the capacity of the twenty-four Class 442 units, which were restricted to the Weymouth and Wareham services, and some of the Southampton ones. All of the Poole trains and the remainder of the Southamptons were handled by Mark 1 units,

The 1999 summer timetable introduced a new hourly service between Waterloo and Wareham. On 1 June, following arrival with the 10.00 ex Waterloo and subsequent reversal, Class 442 unit 2413 departs from Wareham with the 12.36 return working. This view also shows the striking new livery applied to these units from 1998. *Author*

predominantly CIGs and CEPs. It was not unknown for these units to work the faster services on occasions, and for a few years there was a regular Saturday diagram for an eight-car formation, comprising 05.41 Poole to Waterloo, 09.00 Waterloo to Wareham and 11.34 return, 14.30 Waterloo to Weymouth and 17.48 return, and finishing with 21.55 Waterloo to Poole. The author travelled between Waterloo and Southampton Central on the 14.30 Weymouth train one Saturday in 2000, when it was formed of 4-CEP units 1507 and 1537. The Woking to Winchester schedule at that time was particularly stretching – even for a 442 – being just 30 minutes for 42.17 miles, a start-to-stop average of just over 84mph. The CEPs managed the 23-minute Waterloo to Woking timing, and with brisk station work there got away on time at 14.54. The challenging stretch on to Winchester did get the better of them, but not by much – arrival there being just 2 minutes 40 seconds behind time, having actually averaged 77mph. With the slightly easier schedule on to Southampton Central, the arrears were recovered, and departure from there was on time.

This was a fine performance for stock approaching its fortieth birthday, and indeed all of the Mark 1 units operating Bournemouth line services during that period were probably worked harder in terms of sustained high-speed running and daily distances covered than at any time previously in their careers. Nevertheless, efforts were made to squeeze even more out of them.

A number of 4-CIG units had been given the so-called 'Greyhound' modifications in the late 1980s, to improve their performance and reduce journey times over the heavily graded Portsmouth direct line. The modification comprised an additional stage of field-weakening that increased the balancing speed of the motors, improving both acceleration and maximum speed capability. These twenty-two units were renumbered into the 130x series to distinguish them from their unmodified sisters. The seven 4-BEP units that remained after the entire CEP/BEP fleet underwent mid-life refurbishment, and which were allocated to the Portsmouth line, were also given this modification. In 1999, South West Trains acquired eight 4-BIG buffet units from Connex South Central. These were also given the Greyhound modification, had their redundant buffet cars replaced by ex 4-CEP TSO vehicles, and became 4-CIG units 1392–1399. They were turned out very smartly in Stagecoach colours, and with the new red moquette, and became regular performers on the Bournemouth line, where their enhanced performance was

In the late 1990s, South West Trains acquired a number of 4-BIG units from Connex South Central. Ultimately, these were given the 'greyhound' electrical modifications and had their buffet cars replaced by ex 4-CEP TSO vehicles to become 4-CIG units 1392–99. In its unmodified form, unit 2262 departs from Woking with the 08.30 Waterloo to Weymouth service on 1 June 1999. Weymouth services gained a Woking call in the summer timetable that year to connect with the Railair coach service to Heathrow Airport. *Author*

put to good use. A 'convenient' by-product of the supplanting of the buffets by TSOs was that these units had six toilets – surely a record in a four-car set!

Bournemouth line services were 'in the wars' during December 1999, largely as a result of weather conditions. Class 442 unit 2410 suffered a fire in underframe equipment near Eastleigh on the 14th, thought to have resulted from severe arcing caused by icy conditions. Passengers were evacuated and the unit was moved by a diesel shunter to the carriage sidings. On Christmas Eve, there were gales and severe flooding around Lymington Junction, and eight trains were trapped for several hours.

The overall roof at Bournemouth station, which had been in a poor state and supported by scaffolding since suffering damage in the storm of 1987, was fully restored at a cost of £7 million, with contributions from The Railway Heritage Trust and South West Trains. The major work involved replacement of glass and other appropriate materials – the structure is Grade 2 listed – but the opportunity was also taken to make improvements to the platforms, canopies, lighting and brickwork. This was quite a turnaround from the position a year or so earlier, when Railtrack had been considering trying to have the station de-listed so that it could be demolished, claiming that it was beyond economic repair.

11
Into the New Millennium

The initial South West Trains franchise was due to run until 2003, subsequently extended for a year until February 2004. During 2000, negotiations began for a further extension, to 2007. Stagecoach was ultimately the successful bidder again, with the new deal including a requirement to replace all the remaining Mark 1 multiple-units.

The line between Woking and Basingstoke was closed for several hours on 31 January 2000 following a bizarre incident. A diesel engine fell off unit 159 022 as it passed Winchfield in company with unit 159 020, forming the 05.28 Salisbury to Waterloo service. The train was travelling at line speed at the time, and the vehicle involved momentarily derailed, but then rerailed itself. A fuel tank was also ruptured, causing a small fire and discharging its contents on to the track. The leading unit was eventually allowed to continue to London, but 159 020 was later moved to Woking, and then to East Wimbledon depot. The traction current was turned off because of the potential fire risk from the spilt fuel, and disruption continued for much of the day. Subsequent investigation suggested that a seized flywheel may have overstressed the engine support brackets, causing them to fail.

The 2000 summer timetable saw the launch of the Anglia Railways 'Crosslink' service, with six daily trains operating between Colchester/Chelmsford and Basingstoke, with one starting back from Norwich. Operated by Class 170 diesel units, the service took a circuitous route avoiding London, calling at Stratford, Highbury and Islington, West Hampstead, Feltham, Staines, Woking and Farnborough. The inter-regional services had also steadily increased in frequency over the years.

The South Western main line has played host to some unusual services over the years. On 5 April 2000, Class 158 unit 158 838 heads along the down fast line at Old Basing with the 15.17 Wales and West service from Waterloo to Manchester Piccadilly and Pembroke Dock. It is paced on the down slow by 4-CEP unit 1535 leading the 15.15 Waterloo to Southampton. Author

More 'foreigners' on the South Western. Anglia Railways 'Crosslink' service was launched in the 2000 summer timetable. On 2 June, Class 170 unit 170 203 passes Winchfield with the 13.42 Basingstoke to Highbury and Islington service. *Author*

Mark 1 units on a 442 diagram. On a June Saturday in 2000, 4-CEP units 1507 and 1537 depart from Southampton Central with the 14.30 Waterloo to Weymouth service. *Author*

South Central services between Southampton and Bournemouth were withdrawn from the May 2003 timetable. On the last day of through working (Friday, 16 May due to engineering work on the Saturday), 4-CIG unit 1724 arrives at Brockenhurst with the 08.17 Victoria to Bournemouth service. *Author*

Both timetable changes in 2003 saw some adjustments to the intensive service introduced in 1999. Line capacity was coming under some pressure, and reliability was suffering as a result. The worst-affected section was the New Forest stretch between Totton and Brockenhurst, which was handling five trains an hour each way – South West Trains' Weymouth, Wareham and Poole services, the Victoria to Bournemouth train, and a Cross Country service – with only two-aspect signals and long block sections.

An initial step to alleviate this problem was taken in May by cutting back the Victoria to Bournemouth service to Southampton Central, its original destination until 1994. More radical change came in the autumn, with the xx.45 Poole service also terminating at Southampton. This change was slightly more complex, though, in that an hourly shuttle service now ran between Brockenhurst and Wareham, while the former xx.00 Wareham service was cut back to terminate at Poole. In effect, the slower service still ran, but with a section 'cut out' in the middle.

There were some other consequential changes resulting from these adjustments. Chandler's Ford station, on the line between Eastleigh and Romsey, had reopened in May (thirty-four years after closing in 1969), and was served by a diesel unit running between Totton and Romsey via Eastleigh. Together with a stop in the Poole service, this train maintained the service frequency at Totton, and also took up the calls at Redbridge and Millbrook that had been made by some of the xx.45 services. The Poole service also now called at Ashurst New Forest, but not Beaulieu Road, which was left with only a peak-hour service, except on Sundays when a train called every hour.

With the Waterloo to Poole and Victoria to Bournemouth services both now terminating at Southampton Central, the xx.15 from Waterloo was diverted at Eastleigh to Portsmouth Harbour. This train had been one of the few not to serve Southampton Airport Parkway, so its diversion did not affect the overall frequency at this increasingly important station. It also ran non-stop from Waterloo to Basingstoke, but gained a call at Micheldever. This change lost Farnborough its fast service from London, although the xx.45 now called there to maintain the same frequency. The former xx.40 Waterloo to Portsmouth via Eastleigh was cut back to terminate at Basingstoke, along with its half-hourly counterpart.

May 2003 also saw some stock changes on the Lymington branch. Hitherto worked by 4-CIG or 4-VEP units, one of South West Trains' 4-BEP units, 2326, was reduced to three cars by removal of the buffet car, renumbered 1199, and dedicated to the Brockenhurst to Lymington shuttle. With a half-hourly service, this unit was kept very busy for most of the time, except when away at Eastleigh for maintenance. A local guard,

Into the New Millennium

From the 2003 winter timetable, services between Waterloo and Southampton Central no longer called at Farnborough, losing the town its hourly non-stop train to London. On the day before the timetable change, 27 September, 4-CEP unit 1544 finds plenty of custom at Farnborough as it arrives with the 09.00 ex Southampton. *Author*

Another 'loser' in the 2003 winter timetable was Beaulieu Road. Its Monday to Friday off-peak calls were provided by the Waterloo to Poole services, which were cut back to terminate at Southampton Central. On the last day of the summer timetable, 27 September, 4-CIG unit 1885 pauses for custom with the 14.45 Waterloo to Poole service. *Author*

Malcolm Ellis, fabricated a 'Lymington Flyer' headboard, which was regularly carried by 1199 and other Mark 1 units that operated over the line.

A small resignalling scheme was commissioned in the Bournemouth area in December 2003, with a new 'signalling centre' in the former parcels office replacing the existing Bournemouth box and that at Branksome. The new centre controlled the section of line from New Milton to Parkstone, fringing with the signal boxes at Brockenhurst and Poole, and using axle counters for train detection in place of track circuits.

While the 2003 timetable changes had been fairly significant, they looked like minor 'tweaking' compared with the changes that came in in 2004, this year seeing the main timetable change shifted from May to December, to fit in with European practice. Publicised by a 'know your numbers' campaign, South West Trains carried out what was arguably the biggest timetable recast since 1967. Its central feature was a standard service pattern all day on Mondays to Fridays, in place of the previous peak and off-peak arrangements. Trains now departed at the same minutes past *every* hour, with additional peak capacity provided by some additional services inserted into that basic framework.

On the Bournemouth line, the 15-minute interval service had continued to cause some punctuality problems towards Eastleigh and Southampton, where the two faster services 'closed up' on the two slower ones – the xx.45 from Waterloo, for example, was only 3 minutes ahead of the following x1.00 at Southampton Airport Parkway. Any late running by these slower services could hold up the faster trains and result in knock-on delays further west.

The new timetable retained the four trains an hour frequency, but staggered the gaps between them with Waterloo departures as below. Some point-to-point timings were also eased slightly to improve reliability:

xx.05 – Clapham Junction, Basingstoke (43 minutes), Winchester (59 minutes), Southampton Airport Parkway (70 minutes), Southampton Central (77 minutes), Totton, Ashurst New Forest, Brockenhurst (97 minutes), all stations except Sway and Hinton Admiral to Poole (134 minutes);

xx.09 – Woking (26 minutes), Farnborough (36 minutes) Basingstoke (50 minutes), Micheldever (62 minutes), Winchester (72 minutes), Eastleigh (81 minutes), all stations to Portsmouth Harbour (134 minutes).

xx.35 – Woking (25 minutes), Winchester (58 minutes), Southampton Airport Parkway (67 minutes), Southampton Central (74 minutes), Brockenhurst (89 minutes), Bournemouth (105 minutes), all stations except Holton Heath to Weymouth (164 minutes);

The Lymington branch was closed for complete relaying between 5 January and 15 February 2004. On 28 February, 4-CIG unit 1306 runs along the new formation at Lymington Pier as it arrives with the 12.28 shuttle from Brockenhurst. *Author*

Into the New Millennium

In 2003, 4-BEP unit 2326 was reduced to three cars by removal of its buffet car, renumbered 1199, and deployed on the Brockenhurst to Lymington shuttle service. Malcolm Ellis, a guard on the route, made a 'Lymington Flyer' headboard, which was carried by this and other Mark 1 units working the service. On 22 May 2004, the driver fixes the headboard in place at Brockenhurst before departure with the 17.28 to Lymington Pier. *Author*

xx.39 – Clapham Junction, Farnborough (34 minutes), Fleet (40 minutes), Basingstoke (55 minutes), Winchester (74 minutes), Eastleigh (82 minutes), Southampton Airport Parkway (88 minutes) and Southampton Central (95 minutes);

A 10-minute connection was available from the xx.39 into the x1.05 Poole service at Southampton Central, and a similar connection was available from the Weymouth service at Brockenhurst into an hourly stopper to Wareham. Connections were not so good for Lymington Pier, however, where passengers from the Weymouth and Poole services had to wait 24 minutes and 16 minutes respectively. Further up the line, taking the half-hourly slow services between Waterloo and Basingstoke into account, Fleet now enjoyed three trains an hour, and Farnborough four. In the evening peak, the 17.05, 17.35, 18.05 and 18.35 all ran non-stop to Winchester in 55 minutes, and with the exception of the 18.05, divided at Southampton Central into Weymouth and Poole portions. There were also two 'extras', at 17.48 to Southampton Central, and 19.12 to Eastleigh.

The standard pattern in the up direction was as follows:

xx.00 from Weymouth, all stations except Holton Heath to Poole (43 minutes), Bournemouth (54 minutes), Brockenhurst (73 minutes), Southampton Central (88 minutes), Southampton Airport Parkway (98 minutes), Winchester (108 minutes), Woking (140 minutes) and Waterloo (169 minutes);

xx.01 from Poole, all stations except Hinton Admiral and Sway to Brockenhurst (37 minutes), Ashurst New Forest, Totton, Southampton Central (55 minutes), Southampton Airport Parkway (67 minutes), Winchester (77 minutes), Basingstoke (94 minutes), Clapham Junction (131 minutes) and Waterloo (139 minutes);

xx.51 from Portsmouth Harbour, all stations to Eastleigh (47 minutes), Winchester (63 minutes), Micheldever (73 minutes), Basingstoke (84 minutes), Farnborough (100 minutes), Woking (109 minutes) and Waterloo (147 minutes);

xx.55 from Southampton Central, Southampton Airport Parkway (eight minutes), Eastleigh (eleven minutes, and overtaken there by the Poole service), Winchester (28 minutes), Basingstoke (45 minutes), Fleet (58 minutes), Farnborough (64 minutes), Clapham Junction (89 minutes) and Waterloo (99 minutes).

The Wareham to Brockenhurst shuttle ran about midway between the Weymouth and Poole services, and didn't make any particularly convenient connections with either, although as in the down direction, it provided the only service at Holton Heath, Hinton Admiral and Sway. Similarly, the gap between Lymington Pier arrivals and Waterloo departures at Brockenhurst was anywhere between 11 and 19 minutes.

In the morning peak, there were three portion workings. The 06.04 from Bournemouth and 06.11 from Poole combined at Southampton Central, and then called at Southampton Airport Parkway and Winchester, running non-stop from there to Waterloo in 58 minutes. The first Waterloo departure from Weymouth was at 05.54 – this attached to the 06.34 from Poole at Southampton Central and called at Southampton Airport Parkway and Winchester before reaching Waterloo at 08.48, taking 60 minutes for the non-stop run from Winchester. This pattern was repeated half an hour later with a combined 06.24 Weymouth/07.04 Poole, but this made additional calls at Basingstoke and Woking. Other 'extras' included two all stations services from Weymouth to Brockenhurst at 07.25 and 08.25, a train from Southampton Airport Parkway to Waterloo at 06.50, and one from Southampton Central to Waterloo at 07.15

The Saturday service simply followed the same pattern without any of the peak 'extras', while on Sundays the frequency was halved to two trains an hour. From Waterloo, a xx.35 departure called at Woking, Basingstoke, Winchester, Southampton Airport Parkway, Southampton Central, Brockenhurst, New Milton, Bournemouth and all stations except Holton Heath to Weymouth, total journey time being 181 minutes. At xx.54, a train departed for Clapham Junction, Woking, Basingstoke, Micheldever, Winchester and Eastleigh, where it divided. The front portion went forward to Southampton Airport Parkway, Southampton Central and all stations to Bournemouth, taking 150 minutes. The rear portion called at all stations from Eastleigh to Portsmouth Harbour, its journey time being 139 minutes.

Class 442 units continued to work most of the fast Weymouth and Poole services, but the prominence of Mark 1 CIG, CEP and VEP units on the semi-fasts began to diminish, as a result of developments described in the following chapter.

12
The Desiro Era

Class 444 Desiro vehicle fabrication at Siemens' Vienna plant, **12 November 2002.** *Colin J Marsden*

As described earlier, SWTs' initial venture into new stock procurement – with its thirty Class 458 units – was not an unqualified success. However, replacement of the significant fleet of Mark 1 units was now a franchise commitment and so the company, in collaboration with lessor Angel Trains, turned to a different manufacturer, Siemens of Germany. The company already had a proven track record (no pun intended), and after extensive negotiations one of the biggest rolling stock orders post-privatisation was placed with them for the replacement fleet. The stock was based on the company's 'Desiro' template, and eventually comprised 127 four-car Class 450 units for outer-suburban/semi-fast services, and forty-five five-car Class 444 'express' units – 733 vehicles in total, with a contract value of £1.3 billion.

As an 'insurance' against the teething troubles that had beset previous fleets, the development programme included the provision of a 17-mile circuit at Siemens' Wildenrath facility, complete with third rail, on which the units would be tested extensively. The plan was that all the bugs could be ironed out and safety cases satisfied before the units arrived in the UK, so that SWT could set them to work 'out of the box'. It must be said that it was a sound policy that paid off, and while there were still a few early problems, the Desiro fleet was recognised as one of the most reliable straight from service entry. Availability is high, with 117 of the 127 Class 450 units required in service to operate the full timetable, and forty-two units in service out of forty-five for the Class 444s.

Looking at the units in detail, and starting with the four-car 450s, these can be seen primarily as successors to the venerable 4-VEPs. The formation is Driving Motor Open Standard (DMOS(A)), Trailer Composite Open Lavatory (TCOL), Pantograph Trailer Standard Open Lavatory Wheelchair

Class 444 Desiro vehicle assembly at Siemens' Vienna plant, 12 November 2002, with base livery applied and internal fitting out in progress. *Colin J Marsden*

(PTSOLW), and a further DMOS(B). Vehicle length is 20 metres, meaning that twelve-car trains can be accommodated on the same platform lengths as Mark 1 stock, and the two DMOS vehicles weigh in at 46 tonnes each, while the PTSOLW and TCOL are each 35 tonnes. Doors into each vehicle are of the double leaf sliding/plug type, giving a flush bodyside when closed, positioned at the one-third/two-thirds locations. Standard-class seating is generally in a two-plus-three layout, with a mixture of facing bays and airline style, although to facilitate access the latter is restricted to two-seat units. All the airline seats have folding tables in the seat backs. The decision was clearly taken to provide first-class ticket holders with a higher-quality product than the cramped behind-the-cab areas seen on the Class 458s, as well as the 'Electrostar' units being introduced on Southern and South Eastern services. Most of the area between the doors in the TCOL is a dedicated first-class section, with two-plus-two seating in a mixture of facing pairs around tables and airline style, and each end is separated from the rest of the coach by sliding doors and partitions in largely frosted glass, providing a sense of privacy. Between one end of the first-class section and the entrance doors is a four-seat standard class bay, opposite a glass-partitioned guard's compartment – the company having decided to retain guards on all of its trains. These vehicles seat twenty-four first- and thirty-six standard-class passengers, four of the latter in tip-up seats. The PTSOLW has space for two wheelchairs, with nine tip-up seats along the bodysides for use when the areas are not occupied by passengers in wheelchairs; total seating capacity is seventy. There is also an accessible toilet in this area, while a standard one is located in the TCOL vehicle. With seventy seats in both DMOS vehicles, the total unit capacity is 270, thirty-two fewer than the earlier 4-VEP units!

From the traction viewpoint, each DMOS has all axles powered by four Siemens 1TB2016 0GB02 three-phase traction motors, each rated at just over 335hp, giving a total for the unit of 2,682hp, significantly higher than the 1,000hp of the Mark 1 CIG, VEP and CEP units. In one sense, this arrangement harked back to pre-1963 Southern electric units, which also had the

Brand new Desiro – unit 444 001 stands complete at Siemens' Vienna plant, 12 November 2002. *Colin J Marsden*

motor bogies under the driving vehicles. Third-rail pick-up shoes are fitted to both bogies of each DMOS, although in common with most modern electric stock, provision for dual-voltage operation is provided in the form of a lowered roof area for a pantograph on the PTOSLW, together with space under the floor for a transformer, although none of this equipment is actually fitted. The units' maximum speed is 100mph.

The gangway error of the 458s was not repeated; the 450s have 'sliding plate' gangways at the unit ends. These have some similarities with the traditional 'Pullman' type, in that they are held together by spring pressure when units are coupled, and require no manual intervention during coupling. They differ, though, in not taking buffing loads, these being absorbed entirely by the Dellner couplers. Together with a passage through the driving cab, the Southern practice of access throughout a train formed of two or three units continues with the Desiros.

The general arrangements of the Class 444 'express' units owes more than a little to the Class 442 units, not least in their five-car formation, 23-metre vehicle length, location of first-class at one end, and the inclusion of a buffet counter. These units are formed of Driving Motor Open Composite (DMOC), Pantograph Trailer Open Standard Lavatory Wheelchair (PTOSLW), two Trailer Open Standard Lavatory Bicycle (TSOLB, A and B), and Driving Motor Open Standard (DMOS). The gangwayed unit ends are identical to those on the 450s (apart from minor detail differences in gangway design), but there the similarity pretty much ends. Overall, the passenger accommodation is very much to 'main line' standards, with two-plus-two seating in standard class, two-plus-one in first, and most entrance doors into vestibules at the vehicle ends, rather than directly into the passenger saloons. All entrance doors are of single-leaf sliding/plug design, but larger than those on the 442s, and wide enough for easy access with a wheelchair.

In the DMOC, the cab is followed by an entrance vestibule with further glass sliding doors into the first-class section. Thirty-five seats are provided here, the two-plus-one configuration arranged in a mixture of facing bays around tables, and airline style with folding tables in the seat backs. Reading lamps are fitted in the overhead racks, power points are provided for use with laptops and mobile phone chargers, and most of the seats have a limited reclining facility. Seat moquette and carpets are in a patterned dark blue, and window curtains – sliding at top and bottom – are provided.

This section is separated from a small standard-class saloon at the inner end of the vehicle by a frosted glass partition/sliding door arrangement similar to that on the 450s. The standard class saloon contains twenty-four seats in two-plus-two configuration, with eight in facing bays around tables in the centre of the section, and the remainder in airline style. Again, the airline seats have seat-back folding tables, but no reading lights or power points are provided. At the end of this section glass sliding doors give access to the other entrance vestibule. This vehicle weighs 52 tonnes, almost identical to the motor coaches of the former 4-REP units, give or take a little for the metric/imperial conversion.

The PTOSLW has the most complex layout of any vehicles in the unit. Coming through the gangway from the DMOC, there is a pair of seats with a small table on the left, and a standard toilet on the right. Immediately beyond are external doors on either side, followed by a buffet counter on the left. This is much smaller than that on the 442 and, lacking microwave facilities, cannot provide any hot food. It is, however, a positive move that it is included at all and, once the 442s were placed into store, the 444s were the only electric multiple-units in the UK – other than Virgin's 'Pendolinos' – to have such a facility. Vehicle weight is 42 tonnes.

Beyond the buffet is the main standard-class saloon, with a guard's compartment, similar to that on the 450s, on the right. The saloon contains thirty-six seats, predominantly in airline style, but with one pair of facing bays in the centre. In front of the final row of seats are a pair of wheelchair spaces with folding tables mounted in the bodyside for use by passengers in wheelchairs. Full-height glass draft screens separate this area from the second pair of external doors, beyond which is the accessible toilet. This is followed by a further small saloon, comprising a single seat on the right-hand side (to allow access past the toilet), and a pair of four-seat bays around tables. The pantograph space is above this section, so the ceiling is lower than usual and there are no overhead racks.

The two TSOLB vehicles, designated 'A' and 'B', are identical. An entrance vestibule is followed by a saloon seating seventy-six, again mainly in airline layout, but with two pairs of facing bays in the centre of the vehicle. The vestibule at the other end is larger, giving access first to the external doors, and then to a standard toilet on the left, and a stowage area for three bicycles on the right. The 'A' vehicle, marshalled next to the DMOS, turns the scales at 41 tonnes, and the 'B' at 37 tonnes.

Attempting to ensure all the 'bugs' are ironed out before arrival on South West Trains' network – Class 450 outer suburban 'Desiro' 450 001 is put through its paces on the 17-mile test track at Siemens' facility in Wildenrath, Germany, on 19 April 2002. *Colin J Marsden*

Driver's position in a Class 444 Desiro unit. Probably the biggest change from earlier stock is the provision of a combined power/brake controller on the left-hand side – neutral in the centre, back for power, and forward for braking. *Colin J Marsden*

Finally, the DMOS is almost identical in layout to the TSOLB – also seating seventy-six – the main difference being that the space occupied by the toilet and bicycle stowage in those vehicles is taken up by the cab. For some reason, the entrance vestibule at this end, behind the cab, does not have sliding doors into the saloon, but simply full-height glass draught screens behind the last row of seats. Like the other driving car, this vehicle also weighs 52 tonnes. Throughout the unit, standard-class moquette and carpets are identical to that on the 450s, but the two-plus-two seats are wider and have the benefit of folding armrests.

In both the 450s and 444s, the driving cabs have their own dedicated bodyside doors. In the 444s, this avoids the 442 practice of preventing passengers from using the vestibules and external doors behind the cab in use. In practice, however, drivers tend to use these doors only when boarding from ground level. At stations, they normally enter via the passenger and gangway doors.

In terms of traction and electrical equipment, the 444s are very similar to the 450s, and their traction motors have the same rating, giving these units a somewhat poorer power to weight ratio (around 12hp/tonne for the 444s compared with almost 17hp/tonne for the 450s). This is noticeable in a very slightly lower rate of acceleration – not a problem if these units are restricted to longer-distance, limited stop services, but in practice this is not always the case.

Structurally, the Class 450 and 444 vehicle bodies are of aluminium construction, and they are fitted with toothed 'anti-climb' panels low down on the vehicle ends, these being intended to engage with each other in the event of vehicles being forced together in a collision, and prevent one from overriding the other. In a way, this could be seen as a development of the abortive 'cup and cone' devices considered for the Mark 1 units, referred to in an earlier chapter.

The contract to supply the Desiro fleet also included provision of maintenance facilities, including a purpose-built depot. This had to be located reasonably centrally on the routes used by the stock, and both Eastleigh and Fratton were considered but found to be unavailable. Instead, a suitable site was located at Northam with direct access to the Bournemouth main line, on the down side just north of the junction with the branch into Southampton docks. Construction of the depot started in late 2001 and was completed by January 2003, some 22 months earlier than planned. It comprises a four-road

The interior of a TSOLB in a Class 444 'Desiro' unit – slightly utilitarian, perhaps, but the two-plus-two seating is comfortable enough for long journeys, the overhead luggage racks reasonably spacious, and overall the vehicles have a light and airy feel, helped by the large windows. *Author*

carriage shed with an area of 6,415 square metres, a bogie drop facility, wheel lathe, carriage washer (which can operate in temperatures down to -5°C), and facilities for emptying controlled emission toilet (CET) tanks. It is also equipped with sophisticated electronic train monitoring equipment, and the Class 450 and 444 units have technology that allows them to 'talk' to the depot while in service anywhere on the network, which significantly speeds up any fault-finding. There are four reception sidings in addition to the four roads inside the shed, and the depot can accommodate a total of twenty-two Class 450 or 444 units. A battery-operated shunting locomotive allows units to be moved in and out of the carriage shed safely, without the need for a third-rail supply.

Of the initial overall contract value of £1.3 billion, £33.5 million covered the provision of Northam depot and an associated electricity sub-station. The original parties to the deal were SWT, Siemens, and Angel Trains, but as it runs for twenty-five years it includes provision for transfer to another franchisee (a clause that had to be invoked in 2017 after the award of the franchise to a First Group/MTR joint venture).

Desiro power supply upgrade. Existing substations were upgraded, and some new ones provided, such as this one at Oakley, between Worting Junction and Micheldever. Under the 1967 electrification, there was just a track paralleling hut at this location. *Author*

Class 450 Desiro units began operating some Basingstoke services during October 2003, and on 15 October, unit 450 015 was named *Desiro* by Transport Secretary Alistair Darling at Waterloo Station. A few days later, it pauses at Brookwood with the 14.44 Basingstoke to Waterloo service. *Author*

The introduction of the Desiros required some significant upgrades to the traction current supply infrastructure, because of the units' increased power consumption relative to the Mark 1 stock they were replacing. This arose primarily because of the electrical characteristics of the AC traction motors and their control systems. Whereas the DC motors installed in earlier stock drew most current on starting and initial acceleration, with consumption falling as speed rose, the new equipment showed a fairly constant consumption across the speed range. The upgrade work involved increasing the capacity of existing substations as well as providing a number of additional ones, some located at the sites of former track paralleling huts, such as Oakley, Micheldever and Winchester.

At the same time as the introduction of the Desiros, some 'structure' was brought to the South West Trains' livery, with essentially three variations. All have the 'upsweep' on the bodysides and across the roof at unit ends, but otherwise the detail was as follows.

Long-distance stock wore the colours first used on the 442s following their refurbishment in 1998 – a predominantly white bodyside and roof, with a blue band along the windows and along the lower bodyside, the latter embellished by a narrow orange line. The upsweep was red, orange and yellow. As well as the 442s, this scheme graced the 444s, the 159 diesel units and – incorrectly – the 458s. This livery was also worn by the small fleet of Class 170 units that the company operated for some years around the turn of the century.

The 450s, as outer-suburban stock, carried an all-over blue livery of the same shade as the lower bodysides on the express units. The upsweep was identical. Finally, the inner suburban Class 455s wore a striking all-over red, and this necessitated a variation of the upsweep to include a blue area,

The 450s were the first units into service, with a pair operating Alton and Basingstoke services in October 2003. Further introductions followed, the pace dependent on unit deliveries and driver training, with units starting to take over

From the 2004 winter timetable, Waterloo to Southampton Central services began calling at Fleet, giving the town three trains an hour, a direct service to Southampton, and a faster service to London. On 14 December, Class 444 Desiro unit 444 016 makes the Fleet call with the 09.39 Waterloo to Southampton service. *Author*

some Portsmouth line services in early 2004. The 444s began to appear in service from April that year, and were also put to work on Portsmouth line services. This was partly because they were limited to 85mph in their initial weeks of service, and this was the maximum speed limit south of Guildford. More significantly, the intention had always been to concentrate the 444s on this route, allowing withdrawal of the remaining CIG, CEP, BEP and VEP units working the fast services over this route.

February 2004 saw a three-week blockade of the Lymington branch for complete relaying of the track, with a replacement bus service from Brockenhurst. The replacement of largely bullhead rail on wooden sleepers with welded flat bottom track on concrete allowed the overall line limit of 45mph to be raised to 60. This work also saw one of the first uses of new plastic insulator 'pots' for the live rail, in place of the time-honoured ceramic variety.

As Desiro deliveries continued and the units settled into regular service, their sphere of operation widened, with the 450s in particular working throughout South West Trains' network. On the Bournemouth line, 450s and 444s became regular performers on the Poole and Portsmouth via Eastleigh services, together with some of the peak 'extras', such as the 06.50 Southampton Airport Parkway to Waterloo. The 442s remained the mainstay of the 'fast' services to Wareham and Weymouth, but 444s were substituted from time to time.

At the same time the Mark 1 units, which had been on borrowed time for some years, began to disappear. A couple of commemorative events were held, including a 'Slam Door' weekend organised by South West Trains over 14 and 15 August 2004. Mark 1 CIG, CEP and VEP units worked most of the xx.45 Waterloo to Southampton services, together with those to Portsmouth via Eastleigh, and stoppers on the Portsmouth direct line. Passengers buying tickets to London could enjoy unlimited travel all day.

On 5 September, 4-CEP units 2311 and 2313 worked a special return trip from Portsmouth Harbour to Weymouth. The train ran via Fareham and St Denys to Southampton, then on to Bournemouth for a photo-stop. This was followed by a non-stop run to Weymouth, with some very lively running past Wareham and Wool. After a lengthy layover at Weymouth, giving passengers the chance to enjoy the seafront in the sunshine, the return trip followed a similar format, with the addition of a photo-stop at Wareham.

Neither event actually marked the end of Mark 1 EMU operation, with units soldiering on into the following year on both SWT and South Eastern. However, the Bournemouth line did play host to South West Trains' very last main-line Mark 1 working, the 11.35 Waterloo to Bournemouth service on 26 May 2005, which was worked by 'Greyhound' 4-CIG units 1396 and 1398, flanking 4-VEP 3536 to form a twelve-car formation. The train was 'seen off' from Waterloo by SWT chairman, Graham Eccles, and Minister of State from the Department for Transport, Dr Stephen Ladyman. Both made speeches to mark the event, and Dr Ladyman gave a traditional 'right away' with a green flag.

The very last Mark 1 main line working by South West Trains was the 11.35 Waterloo to Bournemouth service on 26 May 2005. The twelve-car train was formed of 4-CIG units 1396 and 1398 flanking 4-VEP 3536, and is seen here racing past Brookwood. Note that unit 1396 carries the 'Lymington Flyer' headboard. *Author*

One exception to the withdrawal of Mark 1 stock involved the Lymington branch. Despite the general withdrawal of such stock, South West Trains purchased a pair of 4-CIG units and sought a special dispensation from Her Majesty's Railway Inspectorate (HMRI) to operate them on the branch. This, they felt, would be a strong selling point, giving this tourist line a 'heritage' feel, and providing a far more cost effective solution than using new stock. The dispensation was granted and so, during 2004 the two units – originally numbers 1883 and 1888 – were reduced to three cars by removal of the TS vehicles, modified to provide wheelchair space and cycle storage, and renumbered 1497 and 1498, this work being carried out at Wimbledon Traincare depot. No. 1497 was repainted in British Rail blue and grey, with full yellow ends and decidedly non-authentic cast aluminium double arrow logos beneath the cab side windows; such an adornment had been carried by the REP, TC and VEP units in their original all-blue livery, but never by CIGs! No. 1498 was turned out in Southern Region green with yellow warning panels covering the lower half of the cab fronts – again, not authentic, but a compromise to meet current safety standards. Each unit carried the name of a former Lymington to Yarmouth ferry – *Freshwater* for 1497,

and *Farringford* for 1498. The units entered service in their modified form on 12 May 2005. The HMRI dispensation obviously came with conditions, specifically that the units were fitted with central door locking, and that they only operated with passengers on board between Brockenhurst and Lymington, although they were permitted to run as empty stock to Wimbledon for maintenance. The units were well received by ordinary passengers and enthusiasts alike on the branch, who could wallow in a little bit of nostalgia during the 10-minute ride!

February 2007 saw all of the Class 442 units taken out of service and placed into storage at Eastleigh. The last scheduled 442 departure from Waterloo was the 18.35 service to Weymouth on 13 January, worked by units 2407 and 2417 (carrying the names *Thomas Hardy* and *Woking Homes* respectively), although some units continued to run on an ad hoc basis until the end of the month. They had been very popular with passengers, and there had been speculation in the enthusiast community for some months beforehand about their impending withdrawal and the reasons for it, but there was no real mystery surrounding it. Their recycled electrical equipment was becoming more difficult to maintain to a reliable standard,

Class 442 sunset, 13 October 2006. With only three months left in scheduled service with SWT, units 2404 (left) and 2405 (right) await departure from Waterloo with, respectively, the 17.05 to Poole, and the 17.35 to Weymouth. *Author*

On the last day of scheduled Class 442 operation, 13 January 2007, unit 2424 awaits departure from Winchester with a service to Waterloo. The later design of jumper cable cover is clearly visible in this view. *Author*

and withdrawal had been an element of Stagecoach's successful bid to retain the franchise in 2007. This obviously required some reshuffling of rolling stock, the most obvious result of which was the transfer of many Class 444s from the Portsmouth to the Bournemouth line, and their replacement by Class 450 units, themselves freed up by the return to service of the Class 458 units, primarily on Waterloo to Reading duties. This caused considerable displeasure among Portsmouth line travellers, who now found most of their services formed of Class 450 units, whose two-plus-three seating was clearly unsuitable for journeys of 90 minutes and upwards.

On the Bournemouth line, all fast services were now in the hands of Class 444s, whose standards of comfort and amenity – two-plus-two standard-class seating, *and* a buffet – were pretty much in line with the 442s that had preceded them. There was still some disquiet though over the number of first-class seats – seventy in a ten-car 444 as against 100 in a ten-car 442 – and there were stories of first-class season ticket holders unable to find a seat in the morning peak at Southampton Airport Parkway and Winchester!

April 2007 saw the first stage of resignalling work between Deepcut and Basingstoke, replacing signalling equipment installed in 1967. This first phase covered the Basingstoke station area, together with the route north towards Reading, and west to beyond Worting Junction, where it joined up with the area resignalled in 1995. It also involved extensive track layout changes at Basingstoke, to provide greater flexibility and reversible working through all four platforms. Control of the resignalled area transferred from the 1967 signal box to a new signalling centre housed in an existing single-storey building just north of the station, although the old box remained in use to control the original signalling eastwards to Deepcut.

Final commissioning of the new equipment in the Basingstoke area took place during a week-long blockade during the Easter holiday period, which saw all lines closed between Winchfield and Micheldever, with bus substitution and some interesting arrangements at the 'boundary' stations. Micheldever, generally a quiet location served by only one train an hour, became a temporary terminus for services from Southampton and points west. Trains arrived on the up side of

Resignalling and track remodelling work in progress at Basingstoke, 10 April 2007. The revised layout came under the control of the new Basingstoke signalling centre (not visible in this view), while the 1967 power signal box, at right, remained in use for three more years to control the line eastwards to Deepcut. *Author*

its single island platform, disgorged their passengers on to waiting buses, and then ran through the facing crossover on to the down line (installed as part of the reversible working arrangements between here and Winchester in 1995). Once clear of the pointwork and beyond the protecting signal, they ran forward on to the down side of the island, ready to pick up passengers arriving by bus and take them south. At times, there were trains standing on both sides of the island, with doors open and passengers boarding or alighting, not something generally seen here!

Winchfield acted as a 'mirror image' of Micheldever, with trains from London terminating and then returning east, but the four-track layout here made things rather more interesting. All trains arrived in the down platform, and once passengers had alighted they ran forward through the facing crossover at the west end on to the down fast line. They then ran back through the station 'wrong line' along the down fast, and through the trailing crossover at the opposite end on to the up fast. The final part of the manoeuvre then involved setting back through the up slow to up fast facing crossover to gain the up platform, ready to collect waiting passengers. The second and third of these movements was not controlled by any fixed signalling, which meant that train crews had to telephone the signaller at Basingstoke for authority. The track layout and higher service frequency meant that Winchfield was busier than Micheldever with, on occasions, trains at both platforms and a third making its way between them.

The December timetable of 2007 brought a major change, in the form of a half-hourly service all the way to Weymouth on Mondays to Saturdays. Trains continued to leave Waterloo at the same xx.05 and xx.35 slots, but the xx.05 was extended from Poole to Weymouth. At the same time, the xx.39 was extended

During the Basingstoke resignalling and remodelling works in April 2007, trains from London terminated and turned back at Winchfield, with bus connections onwards. The turn back manoeuvre was complicated by the need to cross the fast lines in order to reach the up slow. On 10 April, a twelve-car train, with unit 450 091 at the rear, is negotiating the trailing crossover from the down fast to the up fast, before setting back into the up platform to pick up passengers.
Author

Service frequency between Waterloo and Weymouth was doubled to two trains an hour in the 2007 winter timetable, by extending the xx.05 Waterloo to Poole services to the end of the line. On the first Monday of the new service, 10 December, unit 444 012 reaches journey's end with the 08.05 from Waterloo. *Author*

from Southampton Central to Poole (effectively reinstating the slow service that had run until October 2003), allowing the xx.05 to omit calls at Totton, Ashurst New Forest, Branksome and Parkstone, and reach Poole 6 minutes earlier. The xx.35 called only at Poole, Hamworthy, Wareham and Dorchester South between Bournemouth and Weymouth, arriving there in 160 minutes from Waterloo, 4 minutes earlier than before. The different stopping patterns meant that arrivals in Weymouth were some way from half an hour apart, at xx.00 and xx.13, while London-bound departures were similarly staggered, at xx03 and xx.20. Nevertheless, the doubling of the frequency was a significant improvement, and was welcomed by passengers.

One other minor change was also made in this timetable, the diversion of Southern's 14.26 Southampton to Brighton service via Eastleigh, reversing there to take the Botley line to Fareham. The rest of these services ran via St Denys and Netley, the 14.26 taking this unusual route in order to maintain crew knowledge. It also provided the relatively unusual sight of Southern Class 377 units at Eastleigh.

Two milestones were celebrated on the Lymington branch in 2008. The first was the line's designation as a 'Community Rail Partnership' (CRP), a concept under which train operators work together with local communities with the aim of boosting passenger numbers, increasing local economic development, and so safeguarding a line's future. This had first been proposed four years earlier, and was a factor in South West Trains' decision to purchase the two CIG units and promote them as 'heritage' trains on the route.

The second was the 150th anniversary of the line's opening, which was marked on Saturday, 12 July. Branch services during the day were operated by the green CIG unit, 1498, running in multiple with Class 73 locomotive 73 109, *Battle of Britain 50th Anniversary*. During the afternoon there were various activities at Lymington Town station, including entertainment, fund-raising events and refreshment stalls, and a special fare of 20p applied for travel between there and Brockenhurst. SWT Managing Director Stewart Palmer unveiled a plaque to commemorate the anniversary.

Between 5 December 2009 and 10 January 2010 work was carried out to lower the track in Southampton Tunnel so that W10 gauge freight containers could pass through it without restriction. Previously, such containers had been carried on special low-floor wagons that limited train length, and were subject to a 20mph speed limit because of the limited clearance. While the work was in progress, there was a significantly reduced service through the tunnel on Mondays to Fridays, with complete blockades every weekend, and from 28 to 31 December inclusive,

The 150th anniversary of the Lymington branch was commemorated on 12 July 2008, with events at Lymington Town station, and branch services operated by green-liveried 3-CIG 1498 in company with SWT 'Thunderbird' locomotive, 73 109 *Battle of Britain 50th Anniversary*. Complete with 'Lymington Flyer' headboard, the pair prepare to set off from the pier with the 13.44 service to Brockenhurst. *Author*

Like all Southern EMUs before them, the Desiros have had to do battle with severe weather from time to time, and early 2009 saw heavy snowfalls over southern England. On 2 February, unit 444 023 arrives at Winchester with a much delayed Waterloo to Weymouth service. Of particular note is that the train has made use of the bi-directional signalling and run 'wrong line' from Michcldever, not as a direct result of the weather, but because of a failed freight train on the down line further north. *Author*

By early 2010 it was becoming increasingly difficult to keep 3-CIGs 1497 and 1498 in service, particularly because of the problems in sourcing spare parts, and the decision was reluctantly taken to withdraw them. Providing suitable replacement stock proved something of a challenge. The Desiro fleet was heavily utilised during the week, and it was not considered justifiable to tie up a four-car unit on this service all day. The solution was to use a Class 158 two-car diesel unit during the week, and a Class 450 at weekends. Using a diesel unit on an electrified line – especially one that had seen its conductor rails replaced just a few years earlier – seemed a bit of a waste, and there were rumours that the line might be 'de-electrified'. In the event, however, this did not come to pass, and electric units continue to ply the route on Saturdays and Sundays.

Three years after resignalling of the Basingstoke station area, April 2010 saw completion of the scheme, covering the main line east of Basingstoke to the boundary with Woking signalling centre at Deepcut. Once again, a blockade was imposed at Easter, but this time for the holiday weekend only, as most of the fixed signals had already been installed and there were no track alterations involved. The new arrangements provided four-aspect signals throughout, in place of the mix of three- and four-aspects that had been installed in 1967. This increased line capacity, and did away with the uneven signal spacings that had existed around Farnborough and Winchfield as a result of the mix of aspects previously; it was also the final stage in providing continuous four-aspect signalling all the way from Vauxhall to Totton. Shunting signals were provided at Winchfield to facilitate the movements required in connection with the 2007 blockade described above, and a new signal was provided at Farnborough to allow trains to start westbound from the up platform. The 1967 'CLASP' signal box at Basingstoke was finally decommissioned as part of this work, although the building was retained for other purposes.

In 2010 there were also further improvements at Southampton Airport Parkway, with the provision of a new footbridge, complete with lifts. This was located towards the London end of the station, and nearer to the terminal building, giving rise to the airport's famous claim that it has one of the fastest plane to train connections in Europe, at just ninety-nine steps! It made the station fully accessible for disabled passengers, as well as making life easier for all airline passengers with luggage, who no longer had to struggle over the 1966 concrete footbridge to the south, although this remained in use. The work cost around £2 million, part of a £7 million investment in improvements to the airport's overall facilities, including a new multi-storey car park for the station.

The Lymington branch endured a further blockade from 9 January to 29 March 2012, when it was closed beyond Lymington Town station to allow major renovation work to be carried out on the pier. A replacement bus service was provided between Town and Pier stations for the duration of the work.

Easter 2010 saw completion of the Basingstoke to Deepcut resignalling, with removal of the 1967 colour-lights and commissioning of the new equipment. At Fleet on 4 April, an old signal bracket provides a handy seat for one of the S&T staff as it awaits removal. *Author*

Lymington branch 3-CIG unit 1497 *Freshwater*, in BR blue and grey livery, heads away from the Pier station with the 12.44 service to Brockenhurst on 17 April 2010. By this date, 1497 and its sister 1498 were on borrowed time; they were withdrawn less than two months later. *Author*

From the start of the 2010 summer timetable, the Lymington branch 3-CIG units 1497 and 1498 were withdrawn from service. Lack of suitable electric stock resulted in the branch shuttle being operated by Class 158 diesel units during the week, although a Class 450 Desiro was deployed on Saturdays and Sundays. On 1 June 2010, unit 158 886 awaits departure from Lymington Pier with the 15.14 service to Brockenhurst. *Author*

Weymouth and Portland hosted the sailing events during the 2012 Olympic and Paralympic Games, and the railway played its part in moving the large numbers of people attending. South West Trains ran additional services, some diesel operated because of the power supply restrictions west of Branksome, and Cross Country extended a Manchester to Bournemouth service to Weymouth, and ran a round trip to Bournemouth during the layover. On 3 August, South West Trains Class 444 and 159 units stand head to head at Weymouth, while a Cross Country Voyager rests behind. *Author*

The summer of 2012 saw the United Kingdom host the Olympic and Paralympic Games. While events were concentrated on the purpose-built Olympic Park at Stratford, many took place in other venues, with the sailing events based at the Weymouth and Portland National Sailing Academy between 29 July and 11 August. While the A354 road into the town had been improved prior to the Games, there was a strong push to encourage people to use public transport, and the railway was obviously keen to play its part.

A special timetable was put in place during the sailing events, but this took some careful planning on account of the limited line capacity – both in physical terms because of the single-track section between Moreton and Dorchester South, and the traction supply, which limited train length. Additional electric trains ran, generally as eight-car 450 formations to provide as much seating as possible. Other services were operated by Class 159 diesel units, while Cross Country (now operated by Arriva) extended a Manchester to Bournemouth 'Voyager' working to Weymouth, and also provided a round trip to Bournemouth before the return leg from Weymouth to Manchester. For the duration of the events, passenger information screens at stations on the line showed the final destination as 'Weymouth for Portland'.

A further small resignalling scheme was completed in May 2014, covering the area from Poole to Wool. New lightweight LED signals replaced 'conventional' colour-lights, with control from a new 'PW' (Poole-Wool) workstation in the Basingstoke signalling centre. The existing signal boxes at Poole, Hamworthy, Wareham and Wool were abolished, although the western extremity of the line from Moreton onwards remained under the control of Dorchester South signal box. The new signalling made provision for reversible working through Wool on the down line, as well as controlling the connection to the Swanage branch at Worgret Junction, and allowing trains to start in the down direction from the up platform at Wareham.

The Poole to Wool resignalling was commissioned in May 2014, rendering the signal boxes at Poole, Hamworthy, Wareham and Wool redundant, with control transferred to Basingstoke Regional Operating Centre. On 23 May, Class 444 unit 444 001 passes new LED signals and the disused signal box at Wareham as it approaches with the 12.05 Waterloo to Weymouth service. *Author*

The 2015 December timetable introduced some changes to provide more peak-hour seats for commuters. On the Bournemouth line, the 06.50 service from Southampton Airport Parkway to Waterloo, which had for many years been a ten-car Class 444 formation, was now made up to twelve cars of Class 450 stock. This move was not universally welcomed by regular travellers, who preferred the two-plus-two comfort of the 'white trains'.

Bournemouth electrics, fifty years on. On 10 July 2017, Class 444 units 444 001 and 444 039 stand under the original footbridge at Southampton Airport Parkway with, respectively, the 11.20 Weymouth to Waterloo, and the 11.39 Waterloo to Poole. Just visible in the background is the 2010 footbridge – closer to the airport terminal, and with lifts. *Author*

The summer of 2017 saw the lengthening of platforms 1 to 4 at Waterloo, along with associated track layout and signalling changes, to accommodate ten-coach trains. The work involved significant timetable changes and service reductions across the whole network. This view, on platforms 3 and 4, was taken after re-opening on 29 August. *Author*

The South Western Railway franchise was awarded to a First Group/MTR joint venture in August 2017, ending Stagecoach's twenty-one-year tenure. The new operator's livery is seen here on Class 444 unit 444 040 at Fratton, working the 12.48 Fareham to Portsmouth Harbour service on 10 November 2018. *Christopher J Wilson*

13
What Next?

Fifty years on, electric trains continue to ply the route between Waterloo, Bournemouth and Weymouth, carrying commuters and leisure travellers alike. Much has changed – the line is now on its third generation of electric rolling stock, with air-conditioning, wi-fi, AC traction motors and electronic control systems the order of the day. Many stations have service frequencies undreamt of in 1967, and the proportion of commuters and the distances they travel daily have probably increased significantly in the intervening years, with Winchester, Southampton Airport Parkway, Brockenhurst and Bournemouth contributing hugely to season ticket sales. But the one constant throughout has been the oft-maligned, but tried and tested third-rail electrification system.

As mentioned earlier, Bournemouth was the last large-scale main electrification to be carried out using this system, with most of what followed later comprising 'in-filling' schemes, and there has been some debate in recent years over the system's future. In 2012, plans were drawn up for an 'electric spine', primarily for freight services, between Southampton and the Midlands and north, via Basingstoke, Reading, Oxford and Banbury. Some of this will be achieved through the Great Western Main Line electrification, but the plan also envisaged conversion of the Basingstoke to Southampton section from third rail to overhead. Not only would this provide a single electrification system throughout the spine but, it was argued, would also constitute a 'feasibility study' for eventual conversion of the entire Southern third-rail system.

Chapter one describes how overhead electrification was dismissed in the original Bournemouth scheme, largely because of the difficulties of its installation in the suburban area. The network has grown far busier and more complex over the past five decades, and such wholesale conversion now would be a major undertaking. But even converting Basingstoke to Southampton would present challenges, not least in terms of rolling stock provision. With third rail presumably remaining between London and Basingstoke and west of Southampton, dual-voltage stock would be required. While the 'Desiro' stock operating over the route has space for pantographs, transformers and associated equipment, none of this is currently fitted, and so there would be an additional cost in providing it. A decision would then need to be taken on whether to fit it to the whole fleet, bearing in mind that this stock works on other routes across the network, or to create a smaller sub-class of dual-voltage units, with obvious impacts on flexibility. Having said that, the position was perhaps not so different in 1967, with the REP/TC combinations working almost exclusively between Waterloo and Bournemouth.

In the event, while the electric spine is still a 'live' plan, other priorities appear to have pushed the Basingstoke to Southampton proposals a long way down the list, and they are now very much on the 'back burner'. Nevertheless, Network Rail's view is that any future electrification schemes – including any extensions within the former Southern Region area – should almost certainly use the 25kV overhead system. So while the existing third-rail network is probably safe for the foreseeable future, the prospects for any extensions are remote.

The other big challenge facing this route – along with many others – is dealing with ever greater passenger numbers. The short-lived SWT/Network Rail Alliance took some steps to address this problem in the suburban area, extending platforms and sourcing additional rolling stock to provide ten-car trains where possible, but action is required on longer-distance services as well. Some passengers routinely stand from Winchester and sometimes further out in the peak, and overcrowding is not unknown off-peak either, particularly on the first 'cheap-day' trains in the morning. Solutions discussed have involved longer trains or double-decker stock, but none have crystallised into any serious proposals so far.

In terms of rolling stock, the Desiro fleet is coming up to fifteen years old. Historically, passenger stock has had a design life of around thirty to thirty-five years, and much of the Mark 1 stock considerably exceeded this. The trains currently plying the Bournemouth line are therefore barely middle-aged, and should still have a long working life ahead of them, but there are now other factors to consider.

While the vehicle structures and running gear should go on and on, obsolescence is likely to rear its head much sooner in terms of software, systems, and stricter accessibility requirements. One would hope that it would be possible to upgrade and refit as necessary to ensure stock remains 'current' in these areas, but there will inevitably be costs involved, and these are aspects that the planners of the original Bournemouth scheme certainly had no need to take into account!

Finally, two other events had a big impact on the route during August 2017. The first was lengthening of platforms 1 to 4 at Waterloo, with associated layout changes in the station throat – a major undertaking that involved significant service reductions while the work was carried out. The second was the award of the franchise to a joint venture of First Group and MTR (operator of, amongst other things, the Hong Kong metro system), ending Stagecoach's twenty-one-year tenure. However, both of these events, and the developments that will follow from them, take us beyond July 2017, and into the next fifty years.

Appendix 1
1967 Bournemouth Electrification EMUs

4-REP

Unit number	Date into traffic (1)	Buffet car name	Notes
3001	3 Apr 1967	*The Kingston*	(2)
3002	3 Apr 1967	*The Waterloo*	
3003	3 Apr 1967	*The Farnborough*	
3004	5 May 1967	*The Solent*	
3005	5 Jun 1967	*The Hampton Court*	
3006	19 May 1967	*The Bournemouth*	
3007	19 Jun 1967	*The Winchester*	(2)
3008	27 May 1967	*The Sandown*	
3009	19 Jun 1967	*The Wimbledon*	
3010	3 Jul 1967	*The Vauxhall*	
3011	20 Jul 1967	*The Beaulieu*	

Notes

(1) – 'Date into traffic' should not necessarily be read as date into service. Some units needed attention before entering service, and because vehicles were delivered out of sequence many units were temporarily misformed. As detailed in Chapter 5, at least two of these units were not available for service on 10 July 1967.

(2) – TRB 69319 in unit 3001 and TBFK 70807 in unit 3007 were 'prototype' conversions carried out at Eastleigh.

3-TC

Unit number	Date into traffic	Notes
301	3 May 1967	
302	1 Jul 1967	
303	31 Jul 1967	

4-TC

Unit number	Date into traffic (1)	Notes
401	?? Oct 1967	(2)
402	13 Aug 1966	
403	13 Aug 1966	
404	12 Aug 1966	
405	12 Aug 1966	
406	17 Aug 1966	
407	2 Sep 1966	
408	25 Aug 1966	
409	14 Sep 1966	
410	22 Sep 1966	
411	29 Sep 1966	
412	29 Sep 1966	
413	12 Oct 1966	
414	12 Oct 1966	
415	2 Nov 1966	
416	25 Oct 1966	
417	9 Nov 1966	
418	2 Nov 1966	
419	26 Nov 1966	
420	26 Nov 1966	
421	5 Dec 1966	
422	5 Dec 1966	
423	5 Dec 1966	
424	1 Mar 1967	
425	31 Jan 1967	
426	13 Feb 1967	
427	25 Feb 1967	
428	3 Mar 1967	

Notes

(1) – As with the 4-REPs, 'date into traffic' should not necessarily be read as date into service, or date in final formation. Some units were delivered in three-car formation pending completion of the TFK vehicles, and some DTSOs ran for a while in ad hoc formations with REP TRB and TBSK vehicles.

(2) – DTSO 76331, TFK 70844, and TBSK 70812, all in unit 401, were 'prototype' conversions carried out at Eastleigh.

4-VEP

Unit number	Date into traffic	Notes
7701	2 Jun 1967	
7702	5 May 1967	
7703	4 July 1967	
7704	26 May 1967	
7705	6 May 1967	
7706	6 May 1967	
7707	8 Jun 1967	
7708	7 Jun 1967	
7709	16 Jun 1967	
7710	16 Jun 1967	
7711	16 Jun 1967	
7712	16 Jun 1967	
7713	26 Jun 1967	
7714	27 Jun 1967	
7715	4 Jul 1967	
7716	6 Jul 1967	
7717	8 Jul 1967	
7718	8 Jul 1967	
7719	25 Jul 1967	
7720	24 Oct 1967	

These twenty units were built specifically for the Bournemouth electrification, but production of a further 174 units continued from late 1967 until 1974, and they were used throughout the Southern Region, with later examples also working regularly on the Bournemouth line. Nos 7701–20 did not generally stray from South Western Division workings until after the 'facelifting' exercise carried out on the fleet in the late 1980s.

Appendix 2
1974 Additional Bournemouth EMUs

4-REP

Unit number	Date into traffic	Buffet car name	Notes
3012	16 Sep 1974	*The Brooklands*	
3013	16 Oct 1974	*The Avon*	
3014	28 Nov 1974	*The New Forest*	
3015	16 Dec 1974	*The Stour*	

4-TC

Unit number	Date into traffic	Notes
429	28 Jun 1974	Formerly 3-TC unit 301
430	4 Jul 1974	Formerly 3-TC unit 302
431	?? ?? 1974	Formerly 3-TC unit 303
432	21 Feb 1975	
433	2 Feb 1975	
434	18 Jan 1975	

Appendix 3
Class 442 'Wessex Electric' EMUs

Unit number	Date into traffic (1)	Buffet car name and date applied (2)
2401	29 Jan 1988	*Brockenhurst* – 30 Jun 1989
2402	22 Feb 1988	*County of Hampshire* – 7 Apr 1989
2403	10 Mar 1988	*The New Forest* – 22 Apr 1991
2404	8 Apr 1988	*Borough of Woking* – 10 Nov 1995
2405	13 Apr 1988	*City of Portsmouth* – 14 Aug 1992
2406	3 May 1988	*Victory* – 21 Oct 1992
2407	7 May 1988	*Thomas Hardy* – 5 Jun 1990
2408	12 May 1988	*County of Dorset* – 5 Oct 1990
2409	13 May 1988	*Bournemouth Orchestras* – 22 May 1992
2410	17 May 1988	*Meridian Tonight* – 31 May 1994
2411	18 Jun 1988	*The Railway Children* – 30 Jul 2003
2412	23 Jun 1988	*Special Olympics* – 12 Jul 1997
2413	9 Jul 1988	
2414	21 Jul 1988	
2415	4 Aug 1988	*Mary Rose* – 1 Jun 1992
2416	23 Aug 1988	*Mum in a million, Doreen Scanlon* – 10 Mar 1997
2417	26 Aug 1988	*Woking Homes* – 22 Oct 2001
2418	7 Sep 1988	*Wessex Cancer Trust* – 2 Mar 1995
2419	20 Sep 1988	*BBC South Today* – 5 Sep 1989
2420	28 Sep 1988	*City of Southampton* – 6 Dec 1994
2421	25 Oct 1988	
2422	19 Nov 1988	*Operation Overlord* – 27 May 1994
2423	22 Dec 1988	*County of Surrey* – 15 Jul 1992
2424	11 Feb 1989	*Gerry Newson* – 14 Nov 2000

Notes

(1) – 'Date into traffic' here is the date each unit arrived at Bournemouth depot, but further commissioning work was required there before entry to passenger service and, as detailed in Chapter 7, only units 2404–7 were available for service from the start of the new timetable on 16 May 1988.

(2) – Unlike the REP buffet cars, the names (which were carried only on the outside of the Class 442 vehicles), were not applied from the outset, but at various dates during the units' lives, usually in ceremonies at appropriate locations along the line of route.

From late 2006, Class 444 Desiro units began to take over some Class 442 diagrams, and by 3 February the following year, Class 442 operations with South West Trains had ceased completely. Unlike the 4-REP, 4-TC and Class 442 units, however, the Class 444s were not built specifically for the Bournemouth and Weymouth route, and so full fleet details are not provided here.

Bibliography

Books

Balmforth, John. *South West Trains*. Ian Allan. 2011.
Bird, John H. *Southern Steam Sunset*. Runpast Publishing. 1997.
Brown, David. *Southern Electric, Volume 2*. Capital Transport. 2010.
Clough, David N. *The Modernisation Plan*. Ian Allan. 2014.
Freeman Allen, G. *The Southern since 1948*. Ian Allan. 1987.
Glover, John. *Southern Electric*. Ian Allan. 2001.
Green, Chris and Vincent, Mike. *The Network SouthEast Story 1982–2014*. Oxford Publishing Company. 2014.
Longworth, Hugh. *British Railways Electric Multiple Units to 1975*. Oxford Publishing Company. 2015.
Marsden, Colin J. *The DC Electrics*. Oxford Publishing Company. 2009.
Moody, G T. *Southern Electric 1909–1979, 5th edition*. Ian Allan. 1979.
Williams, Alan. *Southern Electric Album*. Ian Allan. 1977.

Magazines

Modern Railways, various issues 1964–1967.
The Railway Magazine, various issues 1966–2013.

Technical Papers and Reports

Various papers of Alan Hawes in NRM Collection ref AL53/36/B/1-6, including paper on *Bournemouth Electrification (710)* by W J A Sykes OBE, C Eng, FI Mech E, FIEE, in *Institution of Locomotive Engineers Journal Vol 58 (Part 5)*, 1968–69.

Electrification: Bournemouth to Weymouth (Dorset) – various papers held by the National Archives under refs AN 199/166 and AN 199/810.

Electrification: Bournemouth – Weymouth (Dorset); new rolling stock – various papers held by the National Archives under refs AN 199/323, AN 199/324 and AN 199/325.

South Hampshire Electrification Scheme: notes of Project Team Meetings 1–12 – held by the National Archives under ref AN 188/50.

Rail Council: Electric and Diesel Traction paper; includes reports on electrification between Royston (Hertfordshire) and Cambridge, and in South Hampshire – held by the National Archives under ref AN 170/495.

Report on the Collision that occurred on 26th January 1985 near Micheldever. HMSO. 1986.

Investigation into the Clapham Junction Railway Accident. Anthony Hidden QC. HMSO. 1989.

Websites

Blood and Custard,
    www.bloodandcustard.com
Signal box prefix codes,
    www.railwaycodes.org.uk/signal/signal_boxes0.shtm

Index

Accidents:
    Chertsey..56
    Clapham Junction........83, 85, 86, 87, 88, 89
    Fleet..60
    Micheldever 61, 62, 63
    Waterloo..52
    West Byfleet 59
    Winchfield 110

Depots and works:
    Bournemouth....7, 15, 16, 18, 64, 66, 80, 86, 99, 102
    Chart Leacon 32, 56
    Eastleigh 18, 29, 30, 34, 56, 64, 79, 80, 83, 91, 107, 112, 121, 125
    Fratton 106, 121
    Northam 121, 122
    Wimbledon 42, 110, 125

First Group/MTR.......................122, 136

Locomotives:
    Class 33 ....8, 9, 30, 32, 33, 34, 37, 39, 42, 43, 45, 52, 53, 55, 56, 58, 60, 62, 63, 64, 66, 68, 77, 90, 99
    Class 47 ....43, 45, 52, 53
    Class 71 ....9, 35, 59, 99
    Class 73 ....8, 22, 26, 32, 33, 34, 35, 37, 42, 45, 53, 60, 61, 77, 79, 91, 97, 129
    Class 74 ....9, 33, 34, 35, 37, 45, 52, 53, 56, 60, 59

Multiple units:
    2-BIL.............................30, 47, 64, 99
    2-EPB...............................42, 56, 58
    2-HAL 30, 31, 47
    2-HAP 9, 30, 31, 42, 46, 47, 53, 77, 91, 92
    3-CEP 112
    3-CIG 125, 129, 131
    3-REP 79
    3-TC......................8, 22, 52, 58
    4-BEP 55, 92, 108, 112, 124
    4-BIG 24, 26, 30, 47, 53, 108
    4-CEP 53, 55, 57, 58, 64, 68, 83, 98, 105, 106, 108, 116, 118, 124
    4-CIG..........24, 26, 30, 47, 53, 55, 57, 58, 61, 64, 91, 92, 97, 102, 105, 108, 112, 116, 118, 124, 125, 129
    4-EPB...42, 57
    4-REP 8, 9, 22, 24, 26, 29, 30, 31, 32, 34, 35, 37, 42, 45, 47, 50, 51, 52, 53, 55, 56, 58, 60, 63, 64, 68, 74, 77, 79, 80, 83, 84, 85, 89, 120, 125, 136
    4-SUB 31, 64, 99
    4-TC 8, 9, 22, 26, 29, 30, 31, 32, 33, 34, 35, 37, 39, 42, 45, 51, 52, 53, 55, 56, 58, 60, 63, 64, 65, 68, 74, 77, 79, 80, 83, 84, 85, 89, 91, 97, 125, 136
    4-VEP 8, 9, 22, 26, 30, 31, 32, 34, 39, 47, 51, 53, 55, 56, 57, 58, 59, 61, 64, 68, 83, 85, 91, 92, 97, 99, 106, 112, 116, 117, 118, 124, 125
    6-REP.......................................83, 92
    6-TC..33
    8-VAB................32, 52, 55, 57, 58, 59
    Class 158 131
    Class 159 ....105, 110, 123, 133
    Class 205 9
    Class 442 ....68, 74, 77, 79, 83, 84, 90, 91, 92, 97, 98, 102, 103, 105, 106, 107, 108, 109, 116, 119, 120, 121, 123, 124, 125, 127
    Class 444 .....117, 119, 120, 121, 122, 123, 124, 127, 134
    Class 450 .....117, 119, 120, 121, 122, 123, 124, 127, 131, 133, 134

Western Region diesel 43

Named trains:
    Bournemouth Belle..........43, 45, 105
    Channel Island Express 102
    Royal Wessex 80, 83, 102

Network SouthEast..........64, 77, 83, 84, 85, 98, 99, 103

People:
    Castle, Barbara MP 46
    Eccles, Graham 124
    Ellis, Malcolm...............................114
    Green, Chris 64, 77
    Hidden, Anthony, QC 86
    Keep, Dudley................................90
    Ladyman, Dr Stephen, MP 124
    McKenna, David............................46
    Moore, John, MP 66
    Palmer, Stewart 129
    Parkinson, Cecil, MP 91
    Pettit, Gordon 66, 90
    Pond, Edward......................69, 107
    Portillo, Michael, MP 90
    Raymond, Sir Stanley 46
    Reid, Sir Robert 66
    Walker, Herbert 5

Signal boxes and signalling centres:
    Adelaide Road...............................60
    Basingstoke 12, 15, 61, 62, 64, 127, 128, 131, 133
    Botley..60
    Bournemouth 114
    Branksome....................................66
    Brockenhurst........................60, 114
    Byfleet Junction 56
    Canute Road 60
    Chapel Crossing 60
    Christchurch.................................57
    Clapham Junction 86, 87
    Dorchester Junction.....................56
    Dorchester South 63, 66, 133
    Eastleigh..........................12, 15, 60
    Esher..56

Fareham 60
Hampton Court Junction 56
Hamworthy 66, 133
Lymington Junction 60
Lymington Pier 15
Lymington Town 15
Millbrook 60
Mount Pleasant Crossing 60
Netley 60
Northam Junction 60
Oatlands 56
Pokesdown 57
Poole 66, 114, 133
Redbridge 60
Romsey 60
Southampton Central 60

St Denys 60
Surbiton 56, 106
Swanwick 60
Totton 60
Waller's Ash East 61
Walton-on-Thames 56
Wareham 66, 133
West Byfleet 56
Weston 61
Weymouth 63, 66
Wimbledon 86
Winchester Junction 15
Woking 15, 59, 106, 131
Wool 66, 133
Woolston 60

South West Trains..............99, 100, 101, 103, 107, 108, 109, 110, 112, 114, 123, 124, 125, 129

Substations 5, 16, 66, 91, 123

Timetables 9, 47, 48, 49, 50, 52, 58, 59, 60, 63, 79, 80, 81, 82, 83, 91, 92, 98, 99, 100, 101, 102, 105, 107, 110, 112, 114, 115, 116, 128, 129, 133, 134

The Southern Way

The regular volume for the Southern devotee

SPECIAL ISSUES

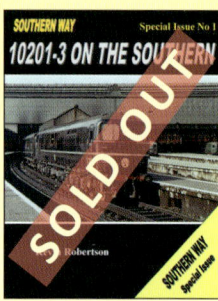
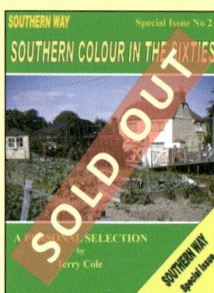
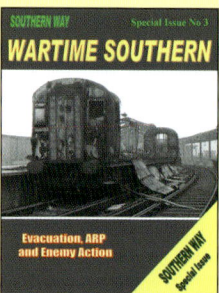

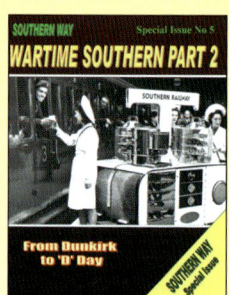
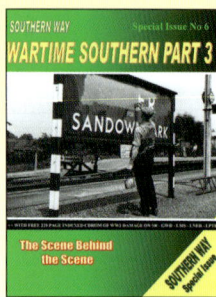
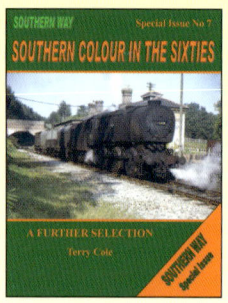
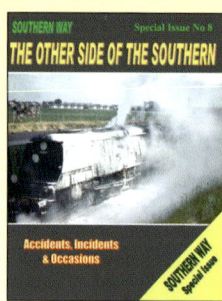
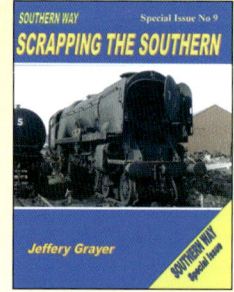
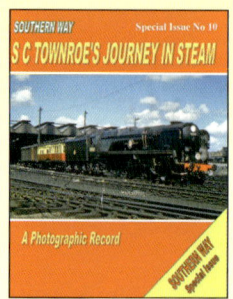

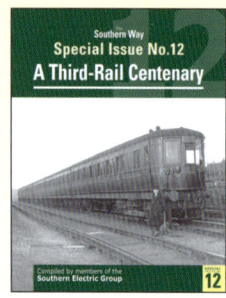
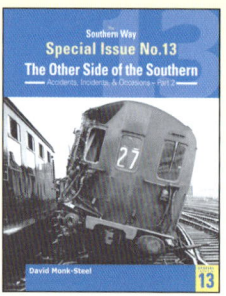

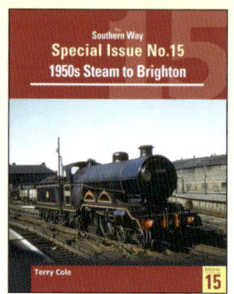

SOUTHERN WAY 'Special Issues'
Nos 3 to 5 £14.95. Nos 6 to 12 £16.50

Orders, subscriptions and sales enquiries to:
Crécy Publishing
1a Ringway Trading Est, Shadowmoss Rd, Manchester M22 5LH

0161 499 0024
www.crecy.co.uk